GW00419168

European Computer Driving Licence®

Syllabus 1.0

Module AM3 - Word Processing

Advanced Level

Using Microsoft® Word 2000

Release ECDL18v5

Published by

CiA Training Ltd
Business and Innovation Centre
Sunderland Enterprise Park East
Sunderland SR5 2TH
Tel: (0191) 549 5002
Fax: (0191) 549 9005
E-mail: info@ciatraining.co.uk
Web: www.ciatraining.co.uk

ISBN 1 86005 048 4

References to the European Computer Driving Licence (ECDL) include the International Computer Driving Licence (ICDL). ECDL Foundation Syllabus Version 1.0 is published as the official syllabus for use within the European Computer Driving Licence (ECDL) and International Computer Driving Licence (ICDL) certification programme.

Approved
Courseware
Advanced
Syllabus AM 3
Version 1.0

Aims

To demonstrate the ability to use a word processing application on a personal computer.

To understand and accomplish more advanced operations associated with the editing, layout, organisation and printing of a word processed document and the use of various elements and special tools.

To demonstrate some of the more advanced features including creating master documents, referencing, working with templates, tables, forms, text boxes and spreadsheets, editing pictures and mail merge documents, creating macros and using advanced printing features.

Objectives

After completing the guide the user will be able to:

- Apply advanced text and paragraph editing

- Create and modify templates

- Track changes and work with comments

- Work with sections and columns

- Create tables of contents and indexes, footnotes and endnotes

- Use field codes, form and document protection

- Modify graphics and apply captions

- Edit mail merge documents

- Work with macros

- Use advanced printing features.

Assessment of Knowledge

At the end of this guide is a section called the **Record of Achievement Matrix**. Before the guide is started it is recommended that the user completes the matrix to measure the level of current knowledge.

Tick boxes are provided for each feature. **1** is for no knowledge, **2** some knowledge and **3** is for competent.

After working through a section, complete the matrix for that section and only when competent in all areas move on to the next section.

Contents

Section 1
Text Editing

By the end of this Section you should be able to:

Apply Text Effects

Animate Text

Use AutoCorrect and AutoFormat

Create AutoText

Change Text Flow and Wrap

Change Text Orientation

Apply Text Design Features (WordArt)

To gain an understanding of the above features, work through the **Driving Lessons** in this **Section**.

For each **Driving Lesson**, read the **Park and Read** instructions, without touching the keyboard, then work through the numbered steps of the **Manoeuvres** on the computer. Complete the **S.A.E.** (Self-Assessment Exercise) at the end of the section to test your knowledge.

Driving Lesson 1 - Text Effects

▣ Park and Read

Various effects such as colour, Shadow, Engrave or SMALL CAPS can be applied to text, making it more eye-catching. Strikethrough is often used in legal documents such as contracts, to suggest removal of a particular clause. Superscript and subscript make the text respectively higher or lower than the other text on the same line, e.g. in mathematical or chemical terms.

⌐ Manoeuvres

1. Open the document **Renaissance** and change the font of all text to **12pt**.

2. Select the title, then select **Format | Font** to display the **Font** dialog box. Make sure the **Font** tab is selected.

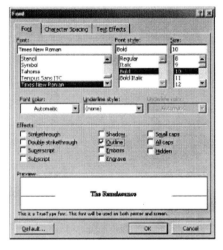

3. Click on the drop down arrow in the **Font color** box. From the colour palette, click on **Dark Red** to change the colour of the title.

[i] *The **Font Color** button,* ⎣A▾⎦*, on the **Formatting** toolbar can be used to change text colour.*

4. More than one effect can be applied at the same time. In the **Effects** area, check the **Outline** option. Notice the **Preview** at the bottom of the dialog box. Click **OK** to apply the effects.

Driving Lesson 1 - Continued

5. Select the subheading **Definition** and select **Format | Font**.

6. Check **Small caps** and **Shadow**, then click **OK** to see the effects.

DEFINITION

7. Scroll down to the section about **Science** and select the sentence beginning **Some people considered...**

8. Select **Format | Font** and check **Strikethrough** then click **OK**.

Science.
Leonardo Da Vinci was a scientist as well as a great artist. He drew many scientific diagrams, varying from the workings of the human body to the working of flying machines (one very like a modern helicopter). ~~Some people considered Da Vinci to be a madman, with hindsight we can say he was more likely to be a genius.~~

9. Leave **Renaissance** open and start a new document.

10. Type in the following text: **The chemical symbol for water is H2O.**

11. Select the **2** and then **Format | Font**.

12. Check **Subscript** and click **OK**.

The chemical symbol for water is H_2O.

13. Press <**Enter**> and type **43 = 64.**

14. This is obviously incorrect. Select the **3** and then **Format | Font**.

15. Check **Superscript** and then **OK**. The sum is now correct: 4 cubed = 64.

The chemical symbol for water is H_2O.
$4^3 = 64$

16. Close the document without saving.

17. Notice in the first paragraph of **Renaissance** that **14th** has **th** in superscript. This feature is applied automatically by *Word*.

The Renaissance

DEFINITION

Renaissance literally means rebirth. It is the name given to the reawakening of interest in the art, literature and science of ancient civilisations like Greece and Rome. The Renaissance began in 14th century Italy, but gradually flowered throughout the rest of Europe. Florence, in Italy, became a major centre of art and learning.

18. Leave the document open for the next Driving Lesson.

Driving Lesson 2 - Animated Text

P Park and Read

Animation can be added to text to create a special effect. Obviously this is a non-printing feature.

Manoeuvres

1. Using **Renaissance**, select the title **The Renaissance** and increase the size to **18pt**.

2. With the text still highlighted, select **Format | Font** and click the **Text Effects** tab.

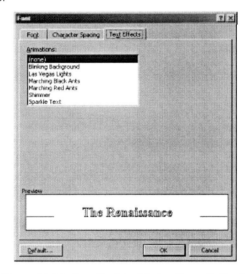

3. Select **Las Vegas Lights** from the list of **Animations**. Notice the **Preview** at the bottom of the dialog box.

4. Click **OK** to apply the text effect.

The Renaissance

5. Give the subheadings various animated effects.

6. Save the document as **Animate** and close it.

Driving Lesson 3 - AutoCorrect

▣ Park and Read

AutoCorrect is a tool that automatically corrects hundreds of common spelling errors and some grammatical ones, such as accidental capitalisation of the second letter in a word.

Manoeuvres

1.   Start a new document and type in the following text, exactly as it appears below:

     the ship sailed past the pier and into teh open sea.

2.   Notice how the errors are automatically corrected. Now type in the days of the week, but do not capitalise the first letter. This error is also automatically corrected.

3.   To see **AutoCorrect's** range, select **Tools | AutoCorrect**. Scroll down the list to see the automatic corrections.

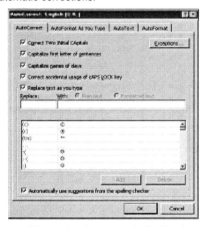

4.   Entries can also be added to the dictionary. In the **Replace** box, enter your initials and in the **With** box, enter your full name. Click on **Add**, then click **OK**.

5.   Now type in your initials, press <**Spacebar**> and they are automatically replaced with your full name.

6.   Select **Tools | AutoCorrect**. Scroll through to find your initials. Click on them once and then **Delete** to remove this entry. Click **OK**.

7.   Close the document <u>without</u> saving.

Driving Lesson 4 - AutoFormat

▣ Park and Read

A document can be automatically formatted after text has been entered. This is called **AutoFormat**. Once a document has been altered in this way, it is still possible to change the formatting.

☞ Manoeuvres

1. Open the document **Papillon**.

2. Above the first paragraph, enter the title **Background** and press **<Enter>**.

3. In the same way, add the title **Escape** to the second paragraph and press **<Enter>**.

4. Make sure there is a space between the first paragraph and the title **Escape**.

5. Select **Format | AutoFormat** to display the **AutoFormat** dialog box.

6. Select **AutoFormat now** and click **OK**. Notice how the document has changed.

7. Print the document and close it <u>without</u> saving, then open **Theft**.

8. Add the following paragraph titles, pressing **<Enter>** after each one and making sure that each title is separated from the previous paragraph by a space: **Chuffington Hall**, **The Thief** and **Case Continues**.

9. **AutoFormat** this document.

10. Print it and close it <u>without</u> saving.

Driving Lesson 5 - AutoText

▣ Park and Read

Phrases (or graphics) that are used frequently can be stored, so that they can quickly be added to a document. The required text is given a name to identify it and can then be called up at any time. This is known as **AutoText**.

Once an **AutoText** entry has been created, it can be inserted into any document. Some **AutoText** entries already exist and can be found within the **AutoCorrect** dialog box.

Manoeuvres

1.   Open the document **Apology**.

2.   Move to the end of the document and select the text **Customer Care Manager**.

3.   Select **Insert | AutoText | New**. The **Create AutoText** dialog box appears.

4.   For the name of the **AutoText entry**, type in **Title**.

5.   Click **OK**. If the following dialog box appears, select **Yes**.

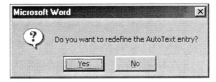

6.   After **at your convenience** in the second paragraph, type **The also wishes to visit you..**

7.   Position the cursor between **The** and **also**, then select **Insert | AutoText | AutoText**.

Driving Lesson 5 - Continued

8. **Title**, the entry created in the last lesson, is available from the list in the **AutoCorrect** dialog box. Scroll down and select it.

9. Click **Insert** to place the **AutoText** in the document.

10. Adjust the spacing if necessary.

11. Move to the end of the document and press **<Enter>**.

12. Start to type **Title** and watch for a yellow box to appear.

13. Press **<Enter>** to complete the entry.

14. To delete the **Title AutoText**, select **Tools | AutoCorrect** and the **AutoText** tab.

15. Scroll down the list and select the **Title** entry.

16. Click **Delete** and then **OK**.

17. Close **Apology** without saving and start a new document.

18. Some words, such as days of the week and months, can be inserted automatically. Start to type **Monday** and when the yellow box appears, press **<Enter>** to complete the entry. This is called **AutoComplete**.

19. Select **Insert | AutoText** and see what entries are available in the menu. Try inserting some into the document.

20. Close the document <u>without</u> saving.

Driving Lesson 6 - Text Flow and Wrap

▣ Park and Read

Click and Type is a feature that allows text, graphics and other objects to be inserted almost anywhere on the page. The formatting required to position the item in the desired place is automatically applied. Text automatically flows and wraps around graphics.

Manoeuvres

1. Open the document **Success**. This was created using the **Click and Type** feature.

2. Close this document and start a new one. Make sure **Print Layout** view is selected, because the feature is only available in this view and in **Web Layout** view.

3. Check that **Click and Type** is turned on. Select **Tools | Options**, click the **Edit** tab and make sure the **Enable click and type** box is checked, then click **OK**.

4. Move the mouse pointer to the centre of the page until it becomes $\underline{\overline{I}}$. The pointer indicates how the item will be formatted.

5. Double click to enable **Click and Type** and insert the **Ringmaster ClipArt** from the **Cartoons** category. If this is not available, use a picture of your choice.

6. Now move the mouse to the right of the graphic until it becomes ▣$\overline{I}$. This means that text entered will be wrapped to the right side of the picture.

7. Double click to enable **Click and Type**, then type in the following text:

    > **Click and Type allows you to insert items anywhere on a page. The only places it cannot be used are: next to floating objects (white handles), in bulleted or numbered lists, where multiple columns are used, to the right or left of indents and to the right or left of pictures which have top and bottom text wrapping.**

8. Click once after typing the text. Now move the cursor down and to the right of the page. When the mouse pointer becomes $\overline{\overline{I}}$. Double click to enable the feature.

Driving Lesson 6 - Continued

i   *If the pointer does not appear like the one in step 8, click once on the page before trying again.*

9. Insert a second piece of **ClipArt**, then click once and move the mouse to the left of the graphic until it becomes I⊞. Double click to enable the feature.

10. Enter a couple of sentences of text about the **ClipArt**.

i   *If the picture is moved, the text is automatically reformatted around it.*

11. Save the document as **Click**, then practice further with the feature.

12. Close the document <u>without</u> saving the changes.

13. Open the document **Papillon** and position the cursor at the beginning of the second paragraph.

14. Insert a clip of a butterfly (look in the **Animals** category).

15. Right click on the picture and select **Format Picture** from the shortcut menu.

16. Select the **Layout** tab. Text wrapping can be changed from here. Select the **Square** option and from **Horizontal alignment** select **Left**.

17. Click **OK**.

18. Try moving the picture around to see the text wrapping change.

19. Close the document <u>without</u> saving.

Driving Lesson 7 - Text Orientation

Park and Read

It is possible to reposition text within a text box or table so that it appears like this or like this .

Manoeuvres

1. Open a new document and select **Insert | Text Box**.

2. Click and drag to draw a rectangular frame anywhere on the page. The cursor will be flashing in the top left corner of the text box.

3. Type the words **Vertical text** into the text box.

4. With the text box still selected, click **Format | Text Direction**. The **Text Direction** dialog box will be displayed.

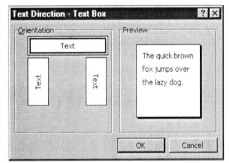

5. Select the lower, left-hand option from the **Orientation** pane and click **OK**.

Driving Lesson 7 - Continued

6.   Close the document <u>without</u> saving.

7.   Start a new document and create a simple table, as shown below.

Fred	Ann	Joe
Left option	Top option	Right option

8.   Select the top left cell.

9.   Select **Format | Text Direction**. The **Text Direction** dialog box will be displayed.

10. Select the lower, left-hand option from the **Orientation** pane and click **OK**. Notice how the alignment buttons on the **Formatting** toolbar have changed.

11. Now select the top right cell (**Joe**) and use the **Text Direction** dialog box to choose the lower, right-hand option from the **Orientation** pane. Click **OK**. Click anywhere outside of the table to remove any selection.

Fred	Ann	Joe
Left option	Top option	Right option

12. Select the cell containing **Ann** and display the **Text Direction** dialog box. Notice that the top option in the **Orientation** pane is selected.

13. Click **Cancel** to close the dialog box without making any changes.

14. Close the document <u>without</u> saving changes.

Driving Lesson 8 - Text Design: WordArt

🅿 Park and Read

Special text effects can be created with the **WordArt** feature. There is a **WordArt Gallery** from which styles can be selected.

Manoeuvres

1. Start a new document and make sure the **Drawing** toolbar is visible.

2. Click the **Insert WordArt** button, , to display the **Gallery**.

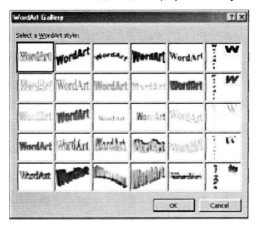

3. Select the fourth style on the fourth row and click **OK**.

4. In the **Edit WordArt Text** dialog box, enter your name. Use the drop down font list to change the font to **Comic Sans MS** and click **OK**.

5. The **WordArt** toolbar appears. Click [Abc] and select an option to change the **WordArt Shape**.

Driving Lesson 8 - Continued

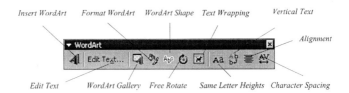

Insert WordArt   Format WordArt   WordArt Shape   Text Wrapping   *Vertical Text*

Alignment

Edit Text   WordArt Gallery   Free Rotate   Same Letter Heights   Character Spacing

6. Make sure the **WordArt** is selected and resize it. Now move it further down the page.

7. Position the mouse over the yellow handle. This changes the skew of the text. Try changing the appearance of the **WordArt** using the handle.

8. Click the **Format WordArt** button,  and change the **Fill Color** to **Yellow** (select the **Colors and Lines** tab).

9. Click **OK**.

10. Select the **Free Rotate** button, and rotate the **WordArt** by dragging a green handle.

11. Click the button again to deselect it.

12. Experiment with the other buttons on the toolbar.

13. To remove the **WordArt** toolbar, click away from the **WordArt**.

14. Close the document without saving.

Driving Lesson 9 - S.A.E.

This is a Self-Assessment Exercise, covering text effects, **AutoFormat**, **AutoText**, text flow, wrap and orientation, text design. Try to complete it without any reference to the previous Driving Lessons in this section.

1. Open the document **Discovery**.

2. Change the body text to **All caps** and the colour to **Blue**.

3. Select the text **glint of gold** in paragraph 2 and apply the **Sparkle Text** effect.

4. Repeat the effect anywhere **gold** or **golden** are mentioned.

5. Draw a text box at the left of the graphic and enter the text **Pyramids at Giza**.

6. Change the orientation of the text in the box so it reads from bottom to top. Resize the box if necessary.

7. Delete the title of the document and replace it with **WordArt** (to read **Tutankhamun**) of your choice. Move the **WordArt** to the top of the document.

8. Save the document as **Discovery2** and close it.

9. Open the document **Cuisine** and **AutoFormat** it. Centre all of the text.

10. Print the document then close it <u>without</u> saving.

11. Start a new document and insert a graphic from the **Photographs** category of the **Insert Clip Art** dialog box.

12. Use the click and type feature to enter a couple of sentences at the very bottom right of the graphic to describe it. Ensure that the text wraps around the graphic.

13. Create an **AutoText** entry, from your first name, to insert **Created for you by *Your name***.

14. Print the document then delete the **AutoText** entry.

15. Close the document <u>without</u> saving.

If you experienced any difficulty completing this S.A.E. refer back to the Driving Lessons in this section. Then redo the S.A.E.

Once you are confident with the features, complete the Record of Achievement Matrix referring to the section at the end of the guide. Only when competent move on to the next Section.

Section 2
Paragraph Editing

By the end of this Section you should be able to:

Shade Paragraphs

Add Borders to Paragraphs

Set Widow and Orphan Controls

Create and Modify Styles

Apply Outline Levels to Styles

To gain an understanding of the above features, work through the **Driving Lessons** in this **Section**.

For each **Driving Lesson**, read the **Park and Read** instructions, without touching the keyboard, then work through the numbered steps of the **Manoeuvres** on the computer. Complete the **S.A.E.** (Self-Assessment Exercise) at the end of the section to test your knowledge.

Driving Lesson 10 - Paragraph Shading and Highlighting

Park and Read

Shading and highlighting with a range of patterns and/or colours can be applied to paragraphs of text. Paragraphs are usually shaded for emphasis, either in shades of grey or colour, while small pieces of text can be highlighted in colour.

Manoeuvres

1. Open **Colorado**.

2. Select the first paragraph and then select **Format | Borders and Shading** and the **Shading** tab.

3. Drop down the **Style** list and select **20%**, then click **OK**.

4. Select the second paragraph and shade it with **Turquoise** (leave the style as **Clear**), ensuring **Apply to** shows **Paragraph**.

5. Try some different **Styles** and **Fills** on this paragraph.

6. From the **Formatting** toolbar, click on the drop down list from the **Highlight** button, and select **Bright Green**.

7. The cursor changes to $\mathcal{A}$. Drag the mouse across the text of the third paragraph to highlight it.

8. To turn off the highlighter, click on the button again.

9. To remove the highlighting, select the third paragraph, then select **None** from the button options.

10. To remove the shading from the document, select the first two paragraphs, then select **Format | Borders and Shading**.

11. Select the **No Fill** option and click **OK**.

12. Close the document without saving.

Driving Lesson 11 - Paragraph Borders

▣ Park and Read

A border can be added to a paragraph to emphasise it. Borders can be added to the whole paragraph or to each line of text within the paragraph.

☞ Manoeuvres

1. Open the document **Definitions** and make sure the cursor is in the first paragraph.

2. Select **Format | Borders and Shading** to display the **Borders and Shading** dialog box. Make sure the **Borders** tab is displayed.

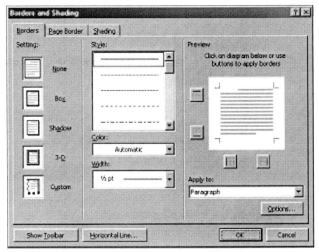

3. Select **Shadow** from the **Setting** area and select a **Color** from the drop down list.

4. Change the border **Width** to **1 pt**.

5. To apply the border to the paragraph, make sure **Paragraph** is selected from the **Apply to** area, then click **OK**.

6. Apply a **Red 2 ¼pt Box** border to the second paragraph.

Driving Lesson 11 - Continued

> A database is a vast store of information consisting of records. A record contains information relating to one person or one company and is made up of individual pieces of information called fields. For example, you may create your records with the following fields: company name, address, telephone number, credit limit, amount owed, payment due, etc. When all the information has been entered, the database can be used to search for particular information. This is called cross-referencing and allows you, for example, to find out at the end of the month who the company owes money to and how much, in order to settle accounts. New information can be entered and the database is updated to include the new data, so that it is always up to date. The computer operated by the DVLA in Swansea (Driving Vehicle Licensing Authority) is an example of a large database. Information relating to every motor vehicle in the U.K. is stored on computer. This information can be accessed to find out who owns a particular car.

> In word processing, a computer behaves like an advanced form of typewriter. Facilities are provided for entering, manipulating, storing and retrieving blocks of text. This means that standard letters and lists of names and addresses can be generated separately, then letters to everyone on the list can be printed without the need to retype the document. The computer retrieves the letter and the first name and address, prints the letter, retrieves the next name and address, changes the information in the letter, prints the next letter and so on. This feature is known as Mail Merge.

7.   Select the third paragraph and apply a **Box** border to each line of text. Leave the other border settings the same, but select **Text** from the drop down list in the **Apply to** area. Click **OK**.

8.   Apply a ¾ **pt Blue Shadow** border to the **Text** of the fourth paragraph.

> A spreadsheet contains rows and columns of boxes called cells in which financial values can be entered. As well as values, text and formulas can be added, text is used to label cells, e.g. 'TOTAL', formula is used to tell the computer how to calculate the value which is to be entered into that cell. Spreadsheets can be used to forecast, for example, what would happen to company profits under various conditions such as an increase in costs, for example.

> Desktop publishing programs are used to produce documents, booklets, magazines, newspapers etc. Obviously it is much easier to do this with a specialised package, than by using traditional methods of cut and paste. Desktop publishing packages allow you to produce text and graphics, which can then be manipulated in the way you want. It is also possible to import existing text and graphics files into a publication.

To remove any border, select the area containing the border and display the
Borders and Shading *dialog box. Select **None** from the **Settings** area. If a border has been applied to text, it will be necessary to select **Text** from the* ***Apply to*** *drop down list before the border can be removed.*

9.   Print the document and close it <u>without</u> saving.

Driving Lesson 12 - Widows and Orphans

Park and Read

The **Widow/Orphan** control prevents *Word* from separating the last line of a paragraph and printing it at the top of a new page (**widow**), or separating the first line of a new paragraph and leaving it at the bottom of the current page (**orphan**). By default, the control is <u>on</u>.

Manoeuvres

1. Open the document **Widows and orphans**.

2. Scroll down until you can see the bottom of page one and the top of page two on the screen.

3. Because the **Widow/Orphan** control is on, two lines of text are kept together at the top of page two.

4. To turn off the control, select the whole document and then **Format | Paragraph** and the **Line and Page Breaks** tab.

5. From the **Pagination** area, remove the check from the **Widow/Orphan control** box.

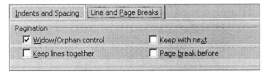

6. Click **OK**.

7. Notice how the final line of text is now left alone at the top of page two – a widow.

8. Turn the control back on by replacing the check in the **Widow/Orphan control** box and click **OK**.

9. Observe how the final line is now joined by the previous one again.

10. Close the document <u>without</u> saving.

Driving Lesson 13 - Creating Styles

▣ Park and Read

Although there are many styles available by default, it is possible to create others. Styles can be created from scratch, or they can be based on other styles.

⌒ Manoeuvres

1. Open **Summary** and add the title **Computer Applications**.

2. From the menu, select **Format | Style** and click on **New** to create a new style.

3. In **Name** enter **MainHead**. Make sure **Based on** shows **Normal**.

4. Click on [Format ▾] and select **Font** from the list.

5. Set the **Font** to **Arial** (or similar), **Font Style** to **Bold** and **Size** to **14**. Click **OK**.

6. Click on **Format** again and select **Paragraph**. From the **Indents and Spacing** tab, select **Centered** from **Alignment** and under **Spacing** change **Before** to **6pt**. Click **OK**.

Driving Lesson 13 - Continued

7. Click **OK** again to finish creating the style.

8. Still within the **Style** dialog box click on **New** again and name the style **Text**. Base it on **Normal**.

 Two styles cannot have the same name. Style names can be up to 253 characters long but cannot include \, { } or ;.

9. Click on **Format**. Set the **Font** to **Times New Roman, Regular, 12**. Click **OK**.

10. Select **Format** again, then **Paragraph**. Set the **Alignment** to **Justified** and the **Left Indent** to **0.6cm**.

11. Click **OK** then **OK** again. Close the **Style** dialog box.

12. Highlight the title **Computer Applications**. Click on the arrow from the **Style** box on the toolbar.

13. Select **MainHead** to format the selected text accordingly.

14. Add the following headings to the paragraphs:

           Paragraph 1 - **Databases**
           Paragraph 2 - **Word Processing**
           Paragraph 3 - **Spreadsheets**
           Paragraph 4 - **Desktop Publishing**

15. Position the cursor within the first paragraph and choose the **Text** style. Repeat for the remaining paragraphs.

i *To create a style using formatted text, select the text, then type the name of the style into the **Style** box on the **Formatting** toolbar,* `Normal ▾`. *Press* *<Enter>*.

16. Highlight the title **Databases**. Use the **Formatting** toolbar to format the text as **Arial, Bold, Italic, 12 pt**.

17. Click on the arrow from the **Style** box and type in **SubHead** to replace the highlighted entry. Press <**Enter**> to create the style based on the selected text.

18. Format the remaining paragraph headings as **SubHead** using the **Style** box drop down list.

19. Save the document as **Applications** and leave it open for the next lesson.

Driving Lesson 14 - Modifying Styles

▣ Park and Read

Once styles have been created and applied they can be changed at any time. A change to a style will change all the text in a document to which that style has been applied, ensuring continuity throughout the document.

☞ Manoeuvres

1. With **Applications** still open from the previous lesson, select **Format | Style**.

2. Scroll down the **Styles** list and select **SubHead**.

3. Click on **Modify** to change the formatting of this style.

4. From the **Modify Style** dialog box, select **Format** then **Font**. Change the **Font** style to **Italic** and check **Small caps** from the **Effects** area.

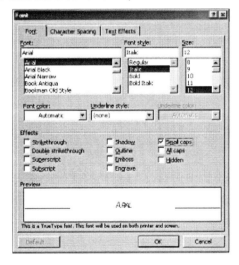

5. Click **OK**.

6. Select **Format | Numbering**, then the **Numbered** tab and choose the second numbering option. Click **OK** then **OK** again.

7. Close the **Style** dialog box. Notice that the text formatted as **SubHead** has now been updated with the changes.

8. Save the document and close it.

Driving Lesson 15 - Outline Level Styles

▣ Park and Read

Once styles have been created and applied to a document, **Outline View** can be used to show the hierarchy of the styles within the document. Within this view, a document can be collapsed to show only those headings contained within it, or expanded so the entire document can be seen. **Outline View** also makes moving around a large document or moving text easier.

Once text has been formatted as a **Heading**, it can be demoted (moved down a Heading) or promoted (moved up by a Heading). All of the selected text will then be reformatted accordingly.

It is easy to reposition text within a document using **Outline View**. If text formatted as a Heading is moved, all text associated with that heading is also moved.

☞ Manoeuvres

1. Open **Stylish**. The heading styles are to have outline levels applied, so that the document can be manipulated in **Outline View**.

2. Modify the **TitleHead**, **MainHead** and **Parahead** styles as follows: select each, in turn, from the **Styles** list in the **Style** dialog box, then click the **Modify** button.

3. Select **Format | Paragraph | Indents & Spacing | Outline level** and apply level **1** to **TitleHead**, level **2** to **MainHead** and level **3** to **Parahead**.

4. Click the **Outline View** button, 🗐 at the bottom left corner of the screen.

5. The **Outlining** toolbar appears. Use **ToolTips** to find out the functions of the buttons.

6. Click on the number **1** on the **Outlining** toolbar. Only the **Title** will be in view.

7. Click on the number **2** and notice the change.

8. Now click on **3** to view all of the **ParaHead** titles.

9. Click back on **2**.

10. Double click on ✿ next to **Types of Printer**. This will expand that title only.

Driving Lesson 15 - Continued

11. Double click again to collapse the text.

12. Save the changes to the document and close it.

13. Open the document **Styles** and view in **Outline** view.

14. To move the heading **Equality**, first select the heading and paragraph associated with it.

15. Collapse the text by clicking ⬛.

16. To move the heading and its associated text upwards, position the cursor within the heading and click on **Move Up**, ⬛, until the text is above **Background**.

17. To make sure the associated text has been moved, double click ⬛ to expand the heading.

i *Text can also be moved by positioning the mouse over the ⊕ next to the required text and dragging it to the new position. Double clicking here also expands and collapses text.*

18. Collapse the heading again and click on **Move Down**, ⬛, to move it back to its original position between **Background** and **Security**.

19. The **Promote** button, ⬛, is used to move the text up a style. The **Demote** button, ⬛, is used to move the text down a style.

20. Select the main title **E-Commerce**, which is **Heading 1** and click **Demote**, ⬛, to change it to **Heading 2**.

21. Collapse all of the remaining paragraphs. Select each of the subheadings in turn (**Heading 2**) and **Demote** them to **Heading 3**.

22. Check what has happened in **Print Layout** view. Switch to **Outline View** and demote the subheadings to **Heading 4**.

23. Now **Promote** the subheadings to **Heading 1** using the **Promote** button, ⬛.

24. Experiment. Try promoting and demoting different headings.

25. Close the document <u>without</u> saving the changes.

Driving Lesson 16 - S.A.E

This is a Self-Assessment Exercise, covering paragraph shading and borders, styles. Try to complete it without any reference to the previous Driving Lessons in this section.

1. Open the document **Computers**.

2. Change the **Style** of the main heading to **Heading1** and the subheadings to **Heading 3**.

3. Create a new style (**Body**) for the body text, based on **Normal**, with the font as **Arial 9pt** and justified.

4. Apply the **Body** style to all body text.

5. In **Outline View**, promote the subheadings to **Heading 2**.

6. Switch to **Print Layout View**.

7. Select the paragraphs about the keyboard and shade them in a colour of your choice.

8. Place a **1½pt black** border around the two paragraphs about memory.

9. Modify the **Body** style font to **Bookman Old Style**, or an alternative font if it is not available.

10. Save the document as **Computers2** and close it.

If you experienced any difficulty completing this S.A.E. refer back to the Driving Lessons in this section. Then redo the S.A.E.

Once you are confident with the features, complete the Record of Achievement Matrix referring to the section at the end of the guide. Only when competent move on to the next Section.

Section 3
Advanced Printing

By the end of this Section you should be able to:

Print Odd and Even Pages

Print Selected Text

Print Specific Pages

To gain an understanding of the above features, work through the **Driving Lessons** in this **Section**.

For each **Driving Lesson**, read the **Park and Read** instructions, without touching the keyboard, then work through the numbered steps of the **Manoeuvres** on the computer. Complete the **S.A.E.** (Self-Assessment Exercise) at the end of the section to test your knowledge.

Driving Lesson 17 - Printing Odd or Even Pages

▣ Park and Read

Rather than print a whole document, it is possible to print only the odd or even pages. This would be done when, for example, odd and even pages were to be printed on different coloured paper, or the document was to be bound and the odd and even pages had to be printed separately.

☞ Manoeuvres

1. Open the document **PC**. This is a six page document.

2. To print only the odd pages, select **File | Print**.

3. From the area at the bottom left of the dialog box, click on the **Print** drop down list and select **Odd pages**.

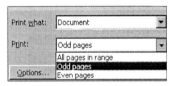

4. Click **OK**.

5. If you have access to different coloured paper, load three sheets into the printer. If not, move to the next step.

6. Now print the even pages only. Select **File | Print** and then **Even pages** from the **Print** drop down list.

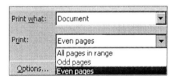

7. Click **OK**.

8. Leave the document open for the next lesson.

Driving Lesson 18 - Printing Selected Text and Pages

▣ Park and Read

Sometimes, you may want to print only small sections of a large document rather than the whole thing. This can be done in a few easy steps.

⌐ Manoeuvres

1. Use the document **PC** for this lesson.

2. Go to page **2**.

3. To print only the section about printers, select the text from **Output: The Printer** to the end of the paragraph about **Laser printers**.

4. Select **File | Print** and from the options in the **Page range** area, click on **Selection**.

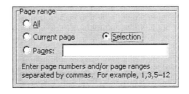

5. Click **OK** to print only the selected text.

6. To print only page **1**, move to the page and select **File | Print** again.

7. From the **Page range** options, select **Current page** and click **OK**.

8. To print the range of pages from **3** to **5**, select **File | Print** again.

9. This time click in the **Pages** option of the **Page range** area.

10. Type **3-5** into the box provided and click **OK**.

11. To print pages **2**, **4** and **6**, select **File | Print** and in **Pages** enter **2,4,6**.

12. Click **OK**.

13. Close the document <u>without</u> saving any changes.

Driving Lesson 19 - S.A.E.

This is a Self-Assessment Exercise, covering printing odd and even pages and selected text. Try to complete it without any reference to the previous Driving Lessons in this section.

1. Open the document **IT**.

2. Print the even pages only.

3. Print only the text about memory.

4. Print pages **1** and **3** only.

5. Close the document <u>without</u> saving.

If you experienced any difficulty completing this S.A.E. refer back to the Driving Lessons in this section. Then redo the S.A.E.

Once you are confident with the features, complete the Record of Achievement Matrix referring to the section at the end of the guide. Only when competent move on to the next Section.

Section 4
Document Layout

By the end of this Section you should be able to:

Add and Delete Section Breaks

Apply Section Shading

Create Multiple Columns in a Document

Modify Column Layout, Width and Spacing

To gain an understanding of the above features, work through the **Driving Lessons** in this **Section**.

For each **Driving Lesson**, read the **Park and Read** instructions, without touching the keyboard, then work through the numbered steps of the **Manoeuvres** on the computer. Complete the **S.A.E.** (Self-Assessment Exercise) at the end of the section to test your knowledge.

Driving Lesson 20 - Adding/Deleting Section Breaks

▣ Park and Read

When certain pages or parts of a document are to be formatted differently from the rest, e.g. page layout or page numbering, sections are created. A document can have as many sections as required.

Manoeuvres

1. Open the document **Retail**. Make sure **Normal** view is selected so you can see the breaks on screen.

2. Position the cursor at the top of **Page 2**.

3. Select **Insert | Break**.

4. From **Section break types**, choose **Continuous**, i.e. it will not start a new page and click **OK**.

> ℹ️ **Even page** and **Odd page Section breaks** will insert a break and start the next section on the next odd or even numbered page of a document.

5. Keep the cursor on the second page. Select **File | Page Setup**.

6. Select the **Paper Size** tab and choose **Landscape** from **Orientation**. Note that **Apply to** shows **This section**.

7. Click **OK** and preview the document. From page **2** onward, the document is in **Landscape**.

8. Position the cursor at the top of page **3** and insert a **Continuous** break.

9. Position the cursor on page **3** and set the orientation to **Portrait**.

10. Click **OK** and preview the document. Set the multiple pages view to **2x2** so that all of the pages can be seen at once.

11. Close the preview. To delete the section break at the top of **Page 2**, position the cursor in front of it.

12. Press <**Delete**>. Preview the document again to see the effect.

13. Close the document without saving.

Driving Lesson 21 - Applying Section Shading

▣ Park and Read

The situation may arise when you want to draw attention to a certain section of a document that is to be handed out. This can be done by applying shading to the section.

Manoeuvres

1. Open the document **PC**.

2. You want to emphasise the section on computer memory to study it for a test tomorrow.

3. Insert continuous section breaks before the following paragraphs:

   Page 2: Internal Memory - RAM and ROM

   Page 2: Output: The Printer

4. Make sure the document is in **Normal View** and highlight the text between the breaks.

5. Select **Format | Borders and Shading** and the **Shading** tab.

6. Choose a colour from the grid and from **Apply to** at the right of the dialog box, make sure **Paragraph** is selected.

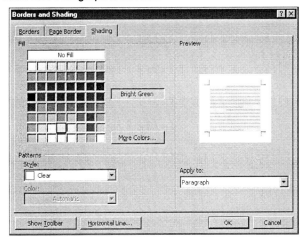

7. Click **OK** to shade the section.

8. Print page **2** only and close the document without saving.

Driving Lesson 22 - Multiple Column Layout

▣ Park and Read

Columns divide the page vertically. Several columns can be created on a page to create a varied effect. Columns can be applied to the whole document, or to certain parts of it.

ℱ Manoeuvres

1. Start a new document and create a **Masthead** (a title that spans the page) with the text **Daily News**.

2. Centre the text and change the font to **Rockwell Extra Bold** (or another bold font if this is not available). Make the text large enough to fill the top line but not so large that it moves on to two lines.

3. Insert a **Continuous Section** break after the **Masthead** to separate it from the text that is to be inserted.

4. Position the cursor underneath the **Masthead** section break (use ▦ if you can't see the break) and click the **Align Left** button, ▤.

5. Select **Insert | File** and insert the data file **Articles**.

6. With the cursor at the beginning of this text, select **Format | Columns**.

7. Select **Two** from the **Presets** area and make sure the **Apply to** area shows **This section**.

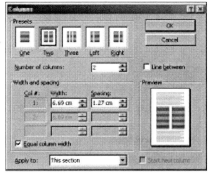

8. Check the **Line between** box to divide the columns with a line and click **OK** to apply the columns (if you are in **Normal View**, *Word* automatically changes to **Print Layout View**).

9. Save the document as **Columns** and leave it open for the next lesson.

Driving Lesson 23 - Modifying Column Layout

Park and Read

Columns can be balanced to divide the text evenly. **Column breaks** are used to move text to the next column.

Manoeuvres

1. Use the document **Columns**. Change the view to **Normal**.

2. Move to the title of the story about the dog.

3. To place this article at the top of the next column, place the insertion point before the **D** of **Dog**.

4. Select **Insert | Break | Column break | OK**. The column break appears as a dotted line across the screen.

5. Switch to **Page Layout** view and notice that the dog article now heads column **2**.

6. Now change the number of columns to **3**. Use a column break to move the **Fundraiser** story to the top of the third column.

7. Print the document.

8. In **Normal** view, click on the first column break and press <**Delete**> to remove it.

9. Delete the remaining column break and switch to **Print Layout** view to see the changes.

10. Close the document without saving to lose the recent changes.

11. Re-open **Columns**.

12. To balance the text in the columns, position the cursor at the end of the text, after the word **proceeds**.

13. Select **Insert | Break | Continuous | OK**.

14. Preview the document. The text should now be equally divided between the two columns.

15. With the cursor in the text, change the number of columns to **3**.

16. Preview the document. The text is still evenly distributed because of the section break.

17. Save the document as **Columns2** and leave it open.

Driving Lesson 24 - Modifying Column Width/Spacing

■ Park and Read

After columns have been applied to a document, it is possible to change the column width and the spacing between columns.

◌ Manoeuvres

1. Using the document **Columns2**, select **Format | Columns**.

2. Remove the check from the **Equal column width** box in **Width and spacing**

3. To change the column widths, amend the measurements in the **Width** boxes to match the following diagram (if these are shown in inches, close the dialog box, select **Tools | Options | General** and select **Centimeters** from the list, then click **OK**).

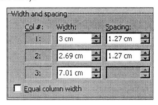

 *The **Spacing** will vary depending on the settings of the printer attached to your PC.*

4. Notice how the **Preview** changes to show the new column widths.

5. Click **OK** to apply the changes.

6. To change the spacing between the three columns, select **Format | Columns** again.

7. Change the **Spacing** measurements to match the following diagram.

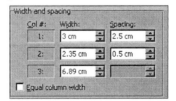

8. Click **OK**.

9. Notice the effect on the document, then close it without saving the changes.

Driving Lesson 25 - S.A.E

This is a Self-Assessment Exercise, covering section breaks and shading, columns. Try to complete it without any reference to the previous Driving Lessons in this section.

1. Open the document **Predators**.

2. Insert **Continuous** section breaks after the **Introduction** section and before the **Conclusion**.

3. Insert a **Next page** section break before the **Senses** section.

4. Apply shading to the **Senses** section only.

5. Apply 2 columns from **Body Form** to **Methods of Reproduction**.

6. Reduce the spacing between the columns to **1cm**.

7. Print the document.

8. Close it <u>without</u> saving.

If you experienced any difficulty completing this S.A.E. refer back to the Driving Lessons in this section. Then redo the S.A.E.

Once you are confident with the features, complete the Record of Achievement Matrix referring to the section at the end of the guide. Only when competent move on to the next Section.

Section 5
Tables

By the end of this Section you should be able to:

Merge and Split Cells

Convert Text to a Table

Sort Data

Perform Calculations

To gain an understanding of the above features, work through the **Driving Lessons** in this **Section**.

For each **Driving Lesson**, read the **Park and Read** instructions, without touching the keyboard, then work through the numbered steps of the **Manoeuvres** on the computer. Complete the **S.A.E.** (Self-Assessment Exercise) at the end of the section to test your knowledge.

Driving Lesson 26 - Merging & Splitting Cells

▣ Park and Read

Cells in a table can be **merged** or **split**. To merge cells means to join two or more cells together to make one large cell. To split cells means to divide a cell into two or more cells.

☞ Manoeuvres

1. In a new document, create a table with **5** columns and **10** rows.

2. Move to the second cell on the top line, select that cell and the cell to the right of it. Select **Table | Merge Cells**. The cells are merged.

> ⓘ *The **Merge Cells** button,* 🔲*, on the **Tables and Borders** toolbar can also be used.*

3. Merge the two cells at the right of the top row then all of the cells on the second row.

4. Merge cells 1 and 2 on rows 3 to 9. This must be done one row at a time.

5. Merge cells 1 to 4 on the bottom row.

6. Your employer wants you to keep a record of daily sales to keep in your Personal Development folder. Enter text into the table until it matches the diagram below.

7. Your employer now decides that product reference numbers should be added to the table. Position the cursor in the cell containing **Product** and select **Table | Split Cells**.

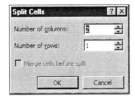

Driving Lesson 26 - Continued

8.　Make sure **2 columns** and **1 row** are selected from the **Split Cells** dialog box and click **OK**.

9.　Enter **Ref.** in the cell to the right of **Product** and split the cells in the six rows below (use the **Split Cells** button, , on the **Tables and Borders** toolbar).

Date	Name		Department		
Product	Ref.	Price	Quantity		Total Price
Grand Total					

i *Cells that have not been merged can still be split.*

10.　Save the document as **Sales Checklist** and close it.

Driving Lesson 27 - Converting Text to a Table

▣ Park and Read

Previously entered text can be converted to table format, providing the text is separated by either commas, tabs or paragraph marks. It may be necessary to remove any extra commas or tabs to reach the required format.

⌒ Manoeuvres

1. Open the document **Diary**. Select all of the text.

2. From the menu select **Table | Convert | Text to Table**.

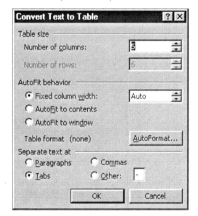

3. The **Number of columns** should be correct. Check that **Separate text at** selection shows **Tabs** and click **OK**.

4. The text will now be in table format. Apply shading to the table, as desired.

5. Save the document as **Converted** and close it.

*To convert a table into text, select the table and from the menu choose **Table | Convert | Table to Text**. From the **Convert Table to Text** dialog box, choose how the text is to be separated. Click **OK**.*

Driving Lesson 28 - Sorting Table Data

▣ Park and Read

Any column can be sorted, with secondary sorts being applied, if required. Ascending or descending sorts can be performed on text or numbers.

☞ Manoeuvres

1. Open the document **Vacation**. This shows the holiday entitlement of staff members.

2. Make sure the cursor is within the table. Select **Table | Sort** to display the **Sort** dialog box.

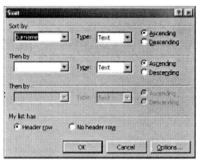

3. Check that **Header** row is checked in the **My list has** area. The **Sort by** choices will now show the column headings.

4. Select **Surname** and **Ascending**. Click **OK** to sort the surnames **A-Z**.

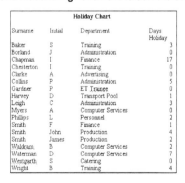

Driving Lesson 28 - Continued

5. Now, with the cursor in the table, select **Table | Sort**. Select **Surname** and **Descending**, then click **OK** to sort the surnames **Z-A**.

Holiday Chart			
Surname	Initial	Department	Days Holiday
Wright	B	Training	4
Westgarth	S	Catering	0
Waterman	D	Computer Services	7
Waldram	B	Computer Services	2
Smith	F	Finance	1
Smith	John	Production	4
Smith	James	Production	2
Phillips	L	Personnel	2
Myers	A	Computer Services	0
Leigh	C	Administration	3
Harvey	D	Transport Pool	1
Gardner	P	ET Trainee	0
Collins	P	Administration	5
Clarke	A	Advertising	0
Chesterton	I	Training	0
Chapman	I	Finance	17
Borland	J	Administration	0
Baker	S	Training	3

6. Again, with the cursor within the table, select **Table | Sort**. From the **Sort by** selection, choose **Days Holiday**, **Descending** and click **OK** (note that the **Type** changes to **Number**).

Holiday Chart			
Surname	Initial	Department	Days Holiday
Chapman	I	Finance	17
Waterman	D	Computer Services	7
Collins	P	Administration	5
Wright	B	Training	4
Smith	John	Production	4
Leigh	C	Administration	3
Baker	S	Training	3
Waldram	B	Computer Services	2
Smith	James	Production	2
Phillips	L	Personnel	2
Smith	F	Finance	1
Harvey	D	Transport Pool	1
Myers	A	Computer Services	0
Westgarth	S	Catering	0
Gardner	P	ET Trainee	0
Clarke	A	Advertising	0
Chesterton	I	Training	0
Borland	J	Administration	0

7. Repeat this sort, adding **Surname**, **Ascending** in the **Then by** section. Select **OK** to sort the list by the amount of holidays, then **A-Z** by surname.

8. Save the document as **Vacation2**, obtain a printed copy and close it.

If lines and borders have already been added to a table, these will be sorted along with the data. It may be prudent to remove all lines and then replace them, if necessary, after sorting.

Holiday Chart			
Surname	Initial	Department	Days Holiday
Chapman	I	Finance	17
Waterman	D	Computer Services	7
Collins	P	Administration	5
Smith	John	Production	4
Wright	B	Training	4
Baker	S	Training	3
Leigh	C	Administration	3
Phillips	L	Personnel	2
Smith	James	Production	2
Waldram	B	Computer Services	2
Harvey	D	Transport Pool	1
Smith	F	Finance	1
Borland	J	Administration	0
Chesterton	I	Training	0
Clarke	A	Advertising	0
Gardner	P	ET Trainee	0
Myers	A	Computer Services	0
Westgarth	S	Catering	0

Driving Lesson 29 - Performing Calculations

▣ Park and Read

Calculations can be carried out within a table. A column of numbers can be summed, or any basic calculation can be performed on the data within the table. Every formula must start with the equals sign **=**. Standard mathematical functions are used to create formulas.

☞ Manoeuvres

1. Create a **5 x 5** table in a new document. Each column in a table is referred to by a letter: **A,B,C,D**, etc., whilst rows are referred to by numbers: **1, 2, 3, 4**, etc. The cell address, e.g. **A1**, is the position where the row and column intersect. It is this cell address that will be used to build formulas, e.g. **=A1 + A2**.

2. In the first column (column **A**) enter a list of four numbers.

3. With the cursor in the last cell of the column, select **Table | Formula**. The formula dialog box suggests a formula that may be appropriate.

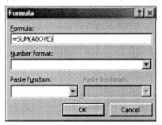

4. In this case **SUM** is required, click **OK** and the sum is complete.

5. Place the cursor in cell **B2**. Select **Table | Formula**. Delete the suggested formula and enter **=a1*a2**. The answer will be displayed.

6. In cell **B3** use the same method to calculate **a2/a1**.

7. To calculate the **Product** of the above two cells, with the cursor in **B4**, open the **Formula** dialog box and remove the suggested formula. Type **=**.

8. From the drop down list under **Paste function**, select **Product**.

9. In the brackets insert **B2,B3**. The formula should read **=PRODUCT(B2,B3)**, the equivalent of **B2*B3**.

10. Click **OK** to perform the calculation. Close the document without saving.

ⓘ *If any numbers are changed the formula is not automatically updated. However, while the formula cell is selected, pressing <F9> will recalculate it.*

Driving Lesson 30 - S.A.E.

This is a Self-Assessment Exercise, covering merging cells, converting text to a table, calculations and sorting data. Try to complete it without any reference to the previous Driving Lessons in this section.

1. Start a new document.

2. Create a new table to match the table below, an invoice (you will need to merge cells).

Invoice				
Ref No	Description	Qty	Price	Total
Subtotal				
VAT				
Total				

3. Print the document and close it <u>without</u> saving.

4. Open the document **Quotas**.

5. Convert the text to a table (separated at tabs).

6. Calculate the total sales for each salesperson.

7. Print the document and close it <u>without</u> saving.

8. Start a new document and create a **4x11** table containing a list of ten types of car.

9. The headings should be **Manufacturer**, **Model**, **Colour** and **Price**.

10. Enter a fictional price for each car.

11. Sort the table in ascending alphabetical order by model.

12. Now sort the table numerically by price, from highest to lowest.

13. Sort the table alphabetically by **Colour**.

14. Save the document as **Car sort** and close it.

If you experienced any difficulty completing this S.A.E. refer back to the Driving Lessons in this section. Then redo the S.A.E.

Once you are confident with the features, complete the Record of Achievement Matrix referring to the section at the end of the guide. Only when competent move on to the next Section.

Section 6
Text Boxes

By the end of this Section you should be able to:

Insert and Delete Text Boxes

Edit Text Boxes

Move and Resize Text Boxes

Apply Borders to Text Boxes

Linking Text Boxes

To gain an understanding of the above features, work through the **Driving Lessons** in this **Section**.

For each **Driving Lesson**, read the **Park and Read** instructions, without touching the keyboard, then work through the numbered steps of the **Manoeuvres** on the computer. Complete the **S.A.E.** (Self-Assessment Exercise) at the end of the section to test your knowledge.

Driving Lesson 31 - Insert/Delete Text Boxes

Park and Read

Placing a **text box** around text allows the text to be positioned anywhere on the page. Other text can be wrapped around text boxes. Text boxes can only be inserted in **Print Layout** view.

Manoeuvres

1. Open the document **PC**.

2. Select the second paragraph, beginning **The second part of the keyboard...**

3. Now select **Insert | Text Box**. The text is placed inside a text box. Notice how the view automatically changes to **Print Layout**.

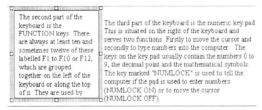

4. Make sure the **Drawing** toolbar is visible (if not, click [icon] on the **Standard** toolbar). Click the **Text Box** button, [icon].

*Drawn text boxes will be placed <u>over</u> text. Create **Text Wrap** using **Format | Text Box | Layout...***

5. At the top of the document, click and drag a box on the page. The cursor flashes in the box, ready for text to be entered.

6. Type in **Text can be entered directly into a text box**.

7. The text box is placed <u>over</u> the text. Select **Format | Text Box** and the **Layout** tab.

8. Select **Tight** from **Wrapping style** and **Right** from **Horizontal alignment** then click **OK**. The text now wraps around the box and is not obscured.

Driving Lesson 31 - Continued

Text can be entered directly into a text box.	INTRODUCTION TO COMPUTERS Input - The Keyboard The keyboard is essentially based on the standard QWERTY keyboard used by typists. The main

differences are the additions made by computer manufacturers. The first thing to notice is that the keyboard has three main sections. The first section is the main QWERTY keyboard which has three extra keys. The most important of these extra keys is usually marked "ENTER" or "RETURN". The

9. The **Text Box** toolbar should be visible. If not, select **View | Toolbars | Text Box**.

10. With the newest text box selected, click on the **Change Text Direction** button, 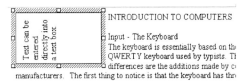, to change the direction of text flow.

INTRODUCTION TO COMPUTERS

Input - The Keyboard
The keyboard is essentially based on th
QWERTY keyboard used by typists. Th
differences are the additions made by c
manufacturers. The first thing to notice is that the keyboard has thr

11. To remove the text box, select the box and press **<Delete>**.

12. Leave the document open for the next Driving Lesson.

Driving Lesson 32 - Manipulating Text Boxes

Park and Read

Text boxes can be resized and moved to any position on the page. It is also possible to edit the text once it has been entered.

Manoeuvres

1. Use the document **PC**, which should still be open from the previous Driving Lesson.

2. To move the text box surrounding the second paragraph, first select it then position the mouse over the shaded edge of the box until a four-headed arrow appears.

3. Click and drag it to a different position. On release, the text on the outside of the box should 'wrap' around it.

4. To change the size of the text box, click on a 'handle' and drag in or out.

5. Notice how changing the shape of the text box changes the flow of the text. By making the text box smaller, some of the text cannot be seen.

6. To edit the text in the text box, with the text box selected, click and drag to select the first sentence.

7. Make the text bold.

8. Delete the words **which are** in the second sentence.

9. Leave the document open for the next Driving Lesson.

Driving Lesson 33 - Adding Borders and Shading

▣ Park and Read

Borders and shading can be applied to a text box in the same way as to other objects.

⌕ Manoeuvres

1. Using the document **PC**, select the text box.

2. Make sure that all of the text it contains can be seen.

3. From the menu, select **Format | Text Box** and the **Colors and Lines** tab.

4. From **Line Color**, select **Aqua** and from **Style** select **1pt**.

5. Select a pale grey from **Fill Color** to apply shading to the text box.

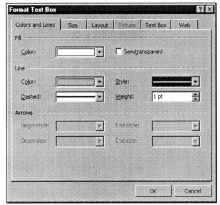

6. Click **OK** to apply the border and shading to the text box.

The second part of the keyboard is the FUNCTION keys. There are always at least ten and sometimes twelve of these labelled F1 to F10 or F12, grouped together on the left of the keyboard or along the top of it. They are used by programs like word processors or spreadsheets to give instructions to the computer. They do not normally produce an effect on the screen but can do in some programs.

7. To remove the text box border and shading, select the text box and then **Format | Text Box** and the **Colors and Lines** tab, then from **Fill Color**, select **No Fill** and from **Line Color** select **No Line**.

8. Click **OK**.

9. Close the document <u>without</u> saving.

Driving Lesson 34 - Linking Text Boxes

▣ Park and Read

Text boxes can be linked to allow the text in one text box to automatically flow into the next box. Linked text boxes can be used to continue related text from one page on to another page.

Manoeuvres

1. Open the document **Predators**.

2. Select the fourth paragraph (**Teeth**) and insert a text box around it.

3. Make the box small enough so that some of the text is not visible.

4. Position the cursor at the end of the document.

5. Click on the **Text Box** button, 🔳, on the **Drawing** toolbar (Select **View | Toolbars | Drawing** if the toolbar is not displayed).

6. Draw a text box at the end of the text.

7. Select the first text box.

8. Click on the **Create Text Box Link** button, 🔳, from the **Text Box** toolbar.

9. Use <**Ctrl End**> to move to the second text box and position the mouse over it.

10. Notice how the mouse changes to a jug.

11. Click in the text box to "pour" the hidden text into the second text box.

12. Change the size of the first text box.

13. Notice how the text in the second text box either increases/decreases accordingly.

14. Experiment by creating another text box and linking that one to the second text box.

15. Save the document as **Boxes** and close the document.

Driving Lesson 35 - S.A.E.

This is a Self-Assessment Exercise, covering inserting, moving and resizing text boxes, adding borders. Try to complete it without any reference to the previous Driving Lessons in this section.

1. Start a new document.

2. Insert a graphic from the **Places** category of **Clip Art**.

3. Draw a text box next to the graphic and enter text about the place you have chosen.

4. Make the text italic and increase the size to **14pt**.

5. Resize the text box to accommodate the text.

6. Apply a green border to the box, line weight **2pt**.

7. Position it at the top of the page, at the right of the graphic.

8. Repeat steps 2 to 6 with a second graphic from the same category.

9. Save the document as **Places**.

10. Close it.

If you experienced any difficulty completing this S.A.E. refer back to the Driving Lessons in this section. Then redo the S.A.E.

Once you are confident with the features, complete the Record of Achievement Matrix referring to the section at the end of the guide. Only when competent move on to the next Section.

Section 7
Graphics & Drawing

By the end of this Section you should be able to:

Modify Graphic Borders

Use Graphic Editing Software

Create a Simple Drawing

Align, Group and Layer Objects

Create a Watermark

Use a Drawing as a Watermark

To gain an understanding of the above features, work through the **Driving Lessons** in this **Section**.

For each **Driving Lesson**, read the **Park and Read** instructions, without touching the keyboard, then work through the numbered steps of the **Manoeuvres** on the computer. Complete the **S.A.E.** (Self-Assessment Exercise) at the end of the section to test your knowledge.

Driving Lesson 36 - Modifying Graphic Borders

 Park and Read

The **Picture** toolbar is used to adjust the formatting, brightness, contrast, etc. of pictures. Pictures can also be given a border, which can then be modified.

Manoeuvres

1. Create a new document and open the **Insert ClipArt** dialog box.

2. Drag any graphic from the **Animals** category into the document, then close the **Insert ClipArt** dialog box.

i *Make sure you drag the graphic, or the **Manoeuvres** will not work.*

3. The **Picture** toolbar should appear automatically. If it is not visible, right click on the picture, then select **Show Picture Toolbar** from the menu.

4. To create a border around the picture, first select it, and then select the **Line Style** button, [≡], from the **Picture** toolbar.

5. Select a border from the drop down list and it will be applied to the graphic.

6. To change the border, select the graphic and then select **Format | Borders and Shading**.

7. Select **Pink** from the **Line Color** area and any other options from the **Line** area.

8. Click **OK** to apply the selections.

9. Practice adding other borders.

10. Close the document without saving.

Driving Lesson 37 - Editing Graphics

Park and Read

After a graphic has been inserted into a document, it can be edited in a special editing mode to change colours, etc.

Manoeuvres

1. In a new document, insert the **mountains** graphic from the **Nature** category in the **Clip Gallery**. Choose a different graphic if this is not available.

2. Right click on the graphic. Select **Edit Picture** from the shortcut menu. The picture opens in an editing mode within *Word*.

3. Click on different areas of the picture in turn to see the available selection areas.

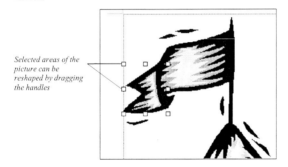

Selected areas of the picture can be reshaped by dragging the handles

4. Select the area shown on the above diagram. To change the colour of this part of the flag, click on the drop down arrow at the right of the **Fill Color** button, ⬛.

5. Select **Dark Green** from the palette.

6. Now select the blue area inside the region just changed. Select **Bright Green** for the **Fill Color**.

7. Continue to change the colour of the flag until you are happy with it.

8. Click Close Picture to exit edit mode and return to the document.

9. Practice editing choosing other images from the **Clip Gallery**.

10. Save the document as **Edit** and close it.

Driving Lesson 38 - Creating a Drawing

▣ Park and Read

The **Drawing** toolbar was used in the introductory ECDL Module 3 to draw basic shapes, but with a little more care, simple drawings can be created.

☞ Manoeuvres

1. Start a new document. You are going to use the drawing tools to make a map of landmarks in a small village. The finished map should look similar to that below.

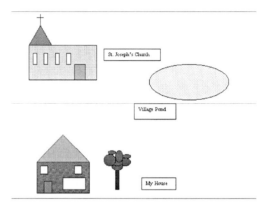

2. Use the **Rectangle** tool, ▢, to draw the main part of buildings. Smaller rectangles will draw windows. Use the **Fill Color** tool to colour the shapes.

3. The cross on the church steeple and the roofs have been drawn with the **Line** tool, ◹. Use this tool for any straight lines.

4. The pond and the green part of the tree have been drawn using different sized ovals. Use the **Oval** tool, ◯, to create circles and ovals.

5. When you have drawn your map, label it with text boxes.

6. Print the document.

7. Save the document as **Village**.

8. Close the document.

Driving Lesson 39 - Aligning, Grouping and Layering Shapes

▣ Park and Read

Once a few objects have been created, they can be aligned and grouped together. Objects can be aligned in relation to each other, or in relation to the page. When objects are grouped, they are treated as a single object and are therefore easier to manage. Objects can be moved about and placed on top of each other, so that some objects are partially covered. Some objects are at the bottom of the pile and others are at the top. Shapes can also be positioned in front of or behind text.

Manoeuvres

1. Start a new document and draw a rectangle, then an oval beneath it.

2. Colour the objects.

3. To select both objects, click on the rectangle, hold <**Shift**> and click on the oval.

4. Click on the **Draw** button, 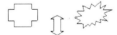. From the list, select **Align or Distribute**, then **Align Left**. The left side of the objects should now be in line.

5. Draw the following three objects using **AutoShapes**. A **Cross** from **Basic Shapes**, an **Up-down arrow** from within **Block Arrows** and **Explosion 2** from **Stars and Banners**.

6. To select all of the objects, click the **Select Objects** button, , then click and drag an imaginary box around all of the objects.

 Objects must be completely inside the box to be selected.

7. All the objects are shown with their handles displayed. From 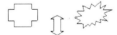, select **Group**. The objects are now grouped together and are treated as a single object. Try resizing and moving them around the screen.

Driving Lesson 39 - Continued

8. To ungroup the objects, click on the object, then select **Draw | Ungroup**.

9. Click on the page to deselect the objects.

10. Select **Draw | Regroup** to regroup the objects. Press <**Delete**> to delete them.

11. Draw an oval and colour it green, a rectangle coloured yellow and a square coloured red.

12. Click and drag the oval until it overlaps the rectangle, then drag the square on top of the oval.

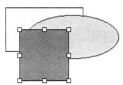

 The positioning of the shapes may be different to the diagram shown above, but the following steps should still work.

13. With the square selected, click the **Draw** button, then select **Order | Send to Back**.

14. To move the square up one layer, make sure it is still selected, click **Draw**, then select **Order | Bring Forward**.

15. Now select the rectangle. Click **Draw** and select **Order | Send Backward**.

16. Draw and colour more objects and practice layering them.

17. Close the document without saving.

18. Open the document **Renaissance** and move to the **Art** paragraph.

19. Draw an oval on top of the text and colour it light blue.

20. With the oval selected, click **Draw**, then **Order | Send Behind Text**.

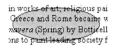

21. To bring the shape back to the front, you must first click the **select Objects** button, [⬚].

22. Now select the shape. Click **Draw**, then **Order | Bring in Front of Text**.

23. Close the document without saving.

Driving Lesson 40 - Creating a Watermark

 Park and Read

A watermark can easily be created on a document, but to appear on every page it must be inserted into the **Header and Footer** area.

Manoeuvres

1. Open the document **Wine**.

2. Select **View | Header and Footer** and make sure that the **Drawing** toolbar is showing.

3. Click the **WordArt** button, and select the second style from the top row of the gallery.

4. Click **OK** and change the **Text** to **Sample**.

5. Click **OK**. Resize the **WordArt** to fill most of the page.

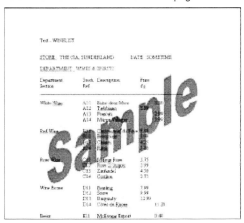

6. Click **Close** on the **Header and Footer** toolbar.

7. The watermark is a little dark. Select **View | Header and Footer** again. Select the **WordArt** and click the **Format WordArt** button, , from the **WordArt** toolbar.

8. On the **Colors and Lines** tab, check **Semitransparent** in the **Fill** area. From **Line Color** select **No Line**. Click **OK** and close the **Header and Footer** toolbar.

9. Print the document and then close it <u>without</u> saving.

Driving Lesson 41 - Using a Drawing as a Watermark

◨ Park and Read

Graphics or drawings can also be used to create a watermark.

◔ Manoeuvres

1. Open the document **CiA**, change to **Print Layout** view and display the **Header and Footer**.

2. Use the drawing tools to draw a simple house.

ⓘ *The drawing can be placed anywhere on the page and will still appear as a watermark where it has been positioned.*

3. Close the **Header and Footer** to see the effect.

4. Now open the **Header and Footer** again and delete the drawing.

5. Select **Insert | Picture | Clip Art**.

6. Choose any graphic and insert it, then close the **Insert Clip Art** dialog box.

7. Click on the graphic, then click the **Draw** button on the **Drawing** toolbar.

8. Select **Text Wrapping | Behind Text**. The graphic can now be moved and resized as required.

9. Right click on the graphic and select **Format Picture** then the **Picture** tab.

10. From **Image Control**, select **Watermark**.

11. Click on the **Layout** tab and from **Horizontal alignment** select **Center** to centre the graphic on the page.

12. Click **OK**.

13. Close the **Header and Footer**.

14. Print the document then close it without saving.

Driving Lesson 42 - S.A.E.

This is a Self-Assessment Exercise, covering editing graphics and modifying borders, drawing and watermarks. Try to complete it without any reference to the previous Driving Lessons in this section.

1. Start a new document.

2. Insert two graphics from the **Cartoons** category of **Clip Art**.

3. Apply borders of your choice to the two graphics.

4. Select one of the graphics to edit.

5. Change some of its colours.

6. Place the edited graphic in the document.

7. Save the document as **Cartoons**.

8. Use the drawing tools to create a face at the end of the document.

9. Print the amended document.

10. Close it <u>without</u> saving.

11. Start a new document and create a watermark from your name.

12. Print the document and close it <u>without</u> saving.

If you experienced any difficulty completing this S.A.E. refer back to the Driving Lessons in this section. Then redo the S.A.E.

Once you are confident with the features, complete the Record of Achievement Matrix referring to the section at the end of the guide. Only when competent move on to the next Section.

Section 8
Referencing

By the end of this Section you should be able to:

Create, Modify & Delete Footnotes & Endnotes

Change Footnote & Endnote Options

Create, Format & Update a Table of Contents

Add & Delete Bookmarks

Create & Delete Cross-references

Add Captions

Change Caption Options

Create & Edit Index Entries

To gain an understanding of the above features, work through the **Driving Lessons** in this **Section**.

For each **Driving Lesson**, read the **Park and Read** instructions, without touching the keyboard, then work through the numbered steps of the **Manoeuvres** on the computer. Complete the **S.A.E.** (Self-Assessment Exercise) at the end of the section to test your knowledge.

Driving Lesson 43 - Creating Footnotes and Endnotes

Park and Read

Footnotes are a formalised way of documenting sources for quotations, facts and ideas in a report. A footnote number is automatically placed in the document next to the text to be referenced. The same number appears at the bottom of the page with details about the source of the information. **Endnotes** perform the same function, but are found at the end of a document.

Manoeuvres

1. Open the document **Discovery**.

2. To create a footnote, position the cursor after **tomb** in the first paragraph and select **Insert | Footnote**.

3. The **Footnote and Endnote** dialog box appears. Make sure that the **Footnote** option is checked and that **Numbering** shows **AutoNumber** then click **OK**.

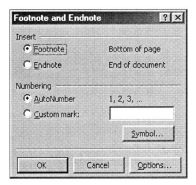

4. The cursor moves to the bottom of the page, ready for the text to be entered. Enter the following text: **Evidence was found of early grave robbers**.

5. Use the scroll bar to move back to the main document and notice how the **reference mark**, the number **1**, has been inserted in the correct place.

Driving Lesson 43 - Continued

6. Move the mouse over the reference mark to display the footnote as a caption.

> Evidence was found of early grave
> robbers.

7. Insert the following footnotes:

    Paragraph **2**, after **Carter**: **Lord Caernarvon financed the dig..**

    Paragraph **3**, after **canopic jars**: **Alabaster or clay pots with the heads of Egyptian deities for lids. Each watched over a particular body part..**

    Paragraph **4**, after **bandaged body**: **Jewels and other precious items were found in the wrappings..**

8. Save the document as **Noted**.

9. Open **Discovery** again.

10. Insert a page break before the fourth paragraph.

11. Position the cursor after **tomb** in the first paragraph and select **Insert | Footnote**.

12. This time select to insert an **Endnote** and click **OK**.

13. Enter the same text as in step **4**.

14. Insert the notes in step **7** as **Endnotes**.

15. Print the document.

16. Save it as **Endnotes** and close it.

Driving Lesson 44 - Modifying/Deleting Footnotes and Endnotes

⊞ Park and Read

Footnotes and endnotes can be edited, formatted and deleted in the same way as normal text. There is a widely observed convention that footnote reference numbers are entered in superscript form.

⌐ Manoeuvres

1. Open the file **Frogs**. This document contains three footnotes.

2. There is a mistake in the second footnote, the magazine referred to is **Frog Monthly** and not **Frog Weekly**. Select **View | Footnotes**.

3. The footnotes appear at the bottom of the screen. The incorrect footnote can now be modified. Edit the text as required.

i *Double click on a reference number in the text to go directly to a footnote or endnote.*

4. Select the first reference mark in the text and then delete it. The footnote text is also removed and the remaining footnotes are automatically renumbered.

i *If a footnote is deleted, the footnote reference mark is not removed. However, if the reference mark is deleted, the corresponding footnote is removed along with it. Great care, therefore, must be exercised when removing footnote reference marks.*

5. Use **Print Preview** to check the appearance of the document.

6. Print a copy of the document and close it <u>without</u> saving the changes.

i *Footnotes may be viewed and edited directly in **Print Layout** view.*

Driving Lesson 45 - Note Options

◪ Park and Read

Footnotes and endnotes can have various formats applied, such as **a,b,c** or **I,II,III**, etc. It is also possible to have footnote numbering restart on each page or section of a document.

☞ Manoeuvres

1. Open the document **Labradors** and place the cursor after **temperament** in the first sentence.

2. Select **Insert | Footnote**. Select to insert a **Footnote** and click the **Options** button.

3. Look at the available options. From **Number format** select a,b,c. Click **OK**.

4. Click **OK** again to insert the following note: **Labradors are especially gentle with children.**

5. Now place the cursor after **waxy near the skin**.

6. Select **Insert | Footnote** and notice that the **AutoNumber** now shows a,b,c – the option selected previously.

7. Click **Cancel** to close the dialog box and close the document without saving.

8. Open the document **Shark**.

9. On page 1, after **Mediterranean** in the second sentence, select **Insert | Footnote** and click **OK**, entering the footnote as **Some specialists believe the Mediterranean to be a nursery for Great White Sharks**.

10. Move to page 2 and the section on **Smell**.

11. Insert a footnote after the first sentence, ending **...through the water**.

12. This time click the **Options** button and from **Numbering** choose to **Restart each page**.

13. Click **OK** then **OK** again. Enter the footnote **A single drop of blood can be detected from miles away**.

14. Notice how the footnote starts at **1**.

15. Close the document without saving.

Driving Lesson 46 - Creating a Table of Contents

▣ Park and Read

When styles have been created and applied to a document, it is a simple task to create **Tables of Contents**, **Indexes**, **Captions**, etc. Once these tables are created, they can automatically be updated, if any of the information is changed.

Manoeuvres

1. Open **Styles**. This document has already been formatted with styles.

2. To create space for the **Table of Contents**, insert 3 blank lines at the beginning of the document and move back to the top.

3. Select **Insert | Index and Tables** and the **Table of Contents** tab.

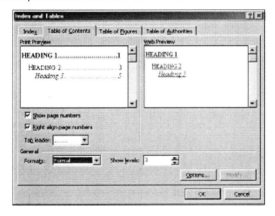

ℹ️ *If the Table of Contents is being created from newly created styles, rather than existing styles, click the **Options** button to specify the order of styles being used. From **Available styles**, remove the level numbers and insert the correct number next to the style. To check that the table shows the correct styles at the correct level, look at the **Preview** before clicking **OK**.*

4. To see different formats applied to the **Table of Contents**, choose each type in turn from the **Formats** drop down list. The preview shows the effects.

Driving Lesson 46 - Continued

5.　Select **Formal**, then click **OK** to create a table of contents.

6.　Leave the document open.

Driving Lesson 47 - Updating a Table of Contents

▣ Park and Read

Once a Table of Contents has been created, it is an easy matter to update it if any changes are made to the contents themselves.

ℭ Manoeuvres

1. Use the document **Styles** for this Driving Lesson.

2. To check that the page numbers are correct, click on a page number in the table of contents.

3. Insert a **Page Break** after the table of contents (**<Ctrl Enter>**). The page numbers are now incorrect.

4. To update the table, place the cursor within it and press **<F9>**.

⚠ *If difficulty is encountered when positioning the cursor, use the cursor keys.*

5. When the **Update Table of Contents** dialog box appears, select the **Update page numbers only** option. Click **OK**.

6. Check the page numbers - they should now be correct.

⚠ *Tables can be automatically updated prior to printing by setting the **Update Fields** option in **Tools | Options | Print**.*

7. Close the document saving the changes.

Driving Lesson 48 - Adding and Deleting Bookmarks

Park and Read

A **Bookmark** is used to move to certain parts of a document very quickly. Once a place within a document has been given a bookmark, it is easier to locate. Text and graphics can be given bookmarks.

Manoeuvres

1.   Open the file **Predators** and position the cursor on page **2**, at the beginning of the **Senses** heading.

2.   From the menu select **Insert | Bookmark**.

3.   Enter **Senses** as the **Bookmark name**.

 A bookmark name can only consist of a single word.

4.   Click **Add** to create the Bookmark.

5.   Create a second, appropriately named bookmark for the **Conclusion** on page **3**.

6.   Insert a graphic of a shark from **Clip Art** after the **Diet** paragraph.

7.   Select the graphic, then select **Insert | Bookmark**.

8.   Enter **sharkpic** as the **Bookmark name** and then click **Add**.

Driving Lesson 48 - Continued

9. Select the first sentence of the **Teeth** paragraph and insert a bookmark named **toothache**.

10. Move the cursor to the beginning of the document.

11. Select **Edit | Go To** to display the **Find and Replace** dialog box.

12. Select **Bookmark** from the **Go to what** box and the **Senses** bookmark from the bookmark name list.

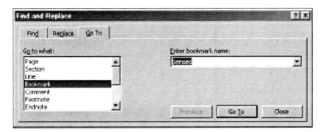

13. Click the **Go To** button to go to the **Senses** section. You may need to move the dialog box to see the result.

14. In the same way, use bookmarks to move to the other bookmarked text and the graphic.

15. To delete the **Senses** bookmark, select **Insert | Bookmark**.

16. Select the **Senses** bookmark from the list.

17. Click the **Delete** button, then click **Close**.

18. Close the document <u>without</u> saving.

Driving Lesson 49 - Cross-Referencing

Park and Read

Cross-referencing is used to refer to an item on another page or elsewhere in a document. It can be used to refer to **Headings, Bookmarks, Captions**, etc. When a cross-reference is created, page numbers, headings, etc., can be automatically updated in the cross-reference, if required.

Manoeuvres

1. Open **Computers** and format **INTRODUCTION TO COMPUTERS** as **Heading 1** and the remaining headings as **Heading 2**. A cross-reference is to be created from the list of the paragraph headings to the paragraph itself.

2. Position the cursor on page 2 at the end of the paragraph named **Internal Memory - RAM and ROM**. Type **(Page** .

3. Select **Insert | Cross-reference**.

4. From **Reference type** choose **Heading**. A list of all the headings formatted as a style can now be seen.

5. From **Insert reference to** select **Page number** and **For which heading** highlight **Processing - The Central Processing Unit**.

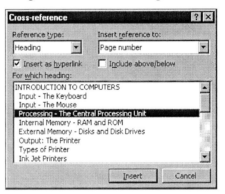

6. Make sure **Insert as hyperlink** is checked, so that a dynamic link between the reference and the referenced text will be created and click on **Insert** to create the cross-reference. Click **Close**.

Driving Lesson 49 - Continued

7. Next to (**Page** the number **1** appears. Enter) after the number 1.

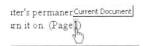

8. Position the mouse pointer over the cross-reference page number, which has just been inserted - a hand appears, because the cross-reference was inserted as a hyperlink. Click once to move to the associated paragraph.

*After moving to a cross-reference, the **Back** button, ⇦ , on the **Web** toolbar can be used to move back to the previous position in the document.*

9. Under the heading **Software - Computer Programs**, find the text **Software takes many forms** and position the cursor after it.

10. Type **(** then select **Insert | Cross-reference**. The **Heading** reference type should still be selected.

11. From **Insert reference to** choose **Heading text**, then from **For which heading**, scroll down the list and choose **COMPUTER APPLICATIONS**. Click **Insert**.

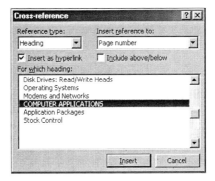

12. Click on **Close**.

13. Enter). Try out the cross-reference.

14. Save the document as **Crossref**.

15. Leave the document open for the next lesson.

*To delete a cross-reference the field codes must be viewed. Select **Tools | Options** and the **View** tab. Check the **Field codes** box and click **OK**. Position the cursor in front of the cross reference to be deleted and press <**Delete**> twice. Remember to turn the field codes off after deleting the cross-reference.*

Driving Lesson 50 - Adding Numbered Captions

▣ Park and Read

Captions can be automatically added to a document so that when a graph, drawing, etc., is inserted, it is automatically numbered. Once captions have been entered in this way a **Table of Figures/Captions** can also be created.

☞ Manoeuvres

1. With **Crossref** still open from the previous lesson, position the cursor before the paragraph **Database** (page 5).

2. Insert a 3 x 3 table and select it.

3. Select **Insert | Caption**. From **Label** choose **Table** and set **Position** to **Above selected item**.

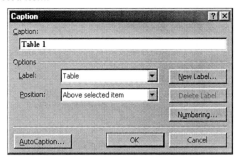

4. Click **OK**. The caption **Table 1** appears above the table.

5. Scroll down the document and position the cursor before the final paragraph, **Spreadsheet**, and insert another 3 x 3 table.

6. Keeping the cursor within the table, select **Insert | Caption**, ensure **Label** shows **Table**.

7. The cursor will be flashing in **Caption** next to **Table 2**. To change the caption text, enter **Sales table** after the existing text. Click **OK**. The caption **Table 2 Sales table** appears.

8. **AutoCaptions** make it possible to automatically insert a caption relating to an object as soon as it is inserted into a document. Select **Insert | Caption** then **AutoCaption**.

Driving Lesson 50 - Continued

9.   Scroll down the list and check **Microsoft Word Table**.

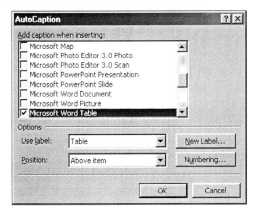

10. Click **OK** and insert a table anywhere in the document. Notice that a caption has automatically been created for it.

> *If the third table is inserted in front of the others, their captions will be renumbered automatically.*

11. Save the document and close it.

> *Once captions have been inserted, the caption style appears in the **Style** list. It can then be formatted as required.*

Driving Lesson 51 - Automatic Caption Options

Park and Read

The previous Driving Lesson showed how *Word* allows captions to be automatically added whenever a table is inserted into a document. **AutoCaptions** can be created for many different types of object.

Manoeuvres

1. Start a new document and select **Insert | Caption**.

2. Click the **AutoCaption** button. To automatically add a caption for each clip that is inserted, scroll down the list and select **Microsoft Word Picture**.

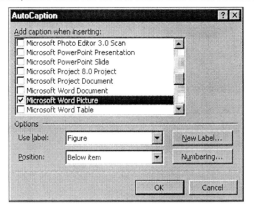

3. To change the caption that appears, click the **New Label** button.

4. Enter the **Label** as **Picture** and click **OK**.

5. Click **OK** again.

6. Insert a graphic from the **Clip Gallery** using the **Insert ClipArt** button. Notice that **Picture 1** appears beneath it.

7. Enter a sentence to describe the graphic, then press **<Enter>**.

8. Insert a second clip. Notice the caption.

9. To stop the automatic captioning, select **Insert | Caption** and the **AutoCaption** button, remove the check from **Microsoft Word Picture** and from **Microsoft Word Table** and click **OK**.

10. Close the document <u>without</u> saving.

Driving Lesson 52 - Creating Index Entries

▣ Park and Read

An **Index** shows the position of selected words or phrases in a printed document. Text required for the index must be marked before the index can be created.

Once styles and captions have been created in a document and cross-referencing and index entries have been marked, it is a simple process to create tables for the entries.

Manoeuvres

1. Open **Computers**. Highlight the first occurrence of the word **keyboard** in the first paragraph.

2. Select **Insert | Index and Tables**. Make sure the **Index** tab is selected. Click on **Mark Entry** to display the **Mark Index Entry** dialog box.

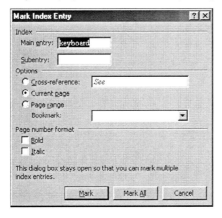

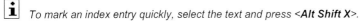

To mark an index entry quickly, select the text and press *<Alt Shift X>*.

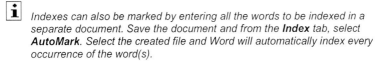

Indexes can also be marked by entering all the words to be indexed in a separate document. Save the document and from the **Index** tab, select **AutoMark**. Select the created file and Word will automatically index every occurrence of the word(s).

Driving Lesson 52 - Continued

3. Ensure **Current page** is selected from **Options**. Check **Italic** in **Page number format**.

4. Click **Mark All** to create an index entry for all occurrences of **keyboard**. The index entry is shown as a field, beginning with **XE**.

    Input—·The·Keyboard¶
    The·**keyboard**{ XE·"keyboard"·\i }·is·essentially·b
    used··by·typists.·The·main·differences·are·the·ac
    The·first·thing·to·notice·is·that·the·keyboard·has

 Mark All marks the first occurrence in each paragraph, so all entries will not be marked. Indexes are case sensitive: Keyboard is not the same as keyboard.

5. Click **Close** to remove the dialog box. Scroll through the document. An index mark appears next to every occurrence of keyboard.

6. Scroll down to the paragraph named **Input - The Mouse** and highlight the word **mouse** on the first line of the paragraph.

7. Press <**Shift Alt X**> to view the **Mark Index Entry** dialog box.

8. Check **Italic for Page number format** then click **Mark All** and **Close** the dialog box.

9. Scroll down the document and create an index entry for **CPU**.

10. Save the document as **Index**.

11. To insert the index, go to the end of the document and press <**Enter**>.

12. Select **Insert | Index and Tables** and the **Index** tab.

13. Select the **Fancy** format.

14. Click **OK** to create an **Index table**.

15. Move to the first index entry and if you don't see the **XE** fields, click **Show/Hide,** ¶ .

16. To edit the index entry, change the text inside the quotation marks to **keyboard, QWERTY**.

ℹ️ *To delete an index entry, select the entire field, including the brackets {}, and then press <Delete>.*

17. To update the index to show the edited entry, click anywhere in the table and press <**F9**>.

18. Close the document without saving the changes.

Driving Lesson 53 - S.A.E.

This is a Self-Assessment Exercise, covering endnotes, tables of contents, indexing, bookmarks, cross-references and captions. Try to complete it without any reference to the previous Driving Lessons in this section.

1. Open the document **IT**.

2. Create endnotes in the **i,ii,iii** style for the following areas:

    QWERTY on the first line – **so called because of the layout of keys on the top row of the keyboard.**

    mouse on the first line of the fourth paragraph – **given this name because its wire resembles a tail.**

3. Move the insertion point back into the document.

4. Amend the second endnote, adding the text **although some may struggle to see the analogy.**

5. At the top of the document, create a table of contents.

6. Insert a page break before **Output: The Printer** on page 2.

7. Now update the table of contents.

8. Create an index at the end of the document, using all headings as index marks.

9. Save the document as **Computers3** and close it.

10. Open the document **Predators**.

11. Create a bookmark for each heading in bold print.

12. Create an additional bookmark to the text **The grey nurse shark** in the **Methods of Reproduction** paragraph.

13. Insert a cross-reference from the first sentence of the **Diet** paragraph to the **The grey nurse shark** bookmark text.

14. Set up **Microsoft Word Picture** automatic captioning.

15. Insert an appropriate graphic from **Clip Art** after the **Teeth** section and a second graphic after the **Sight** paragraph.

16. Save the document as **Jaws** and close it.

If you experienced any difficulty completing this S.A.E. refer back to the Driving Lessons in this section. Then redo the S.A.E.

Once you are confident with the features, complete the Record of Achievement Matrix referring to the section at the end of the guide. Only when competent move on to the next Section.

Section 9
Templates

By the end of this Section you should be able to:

Create a New Template

Modify a Template

Attach a Template to a Document

To gain an understanding of the above features, work through the **Driving Lessons** in this **Section**.

For each **Driving Lesson**, read the **Park and Read** instructions, without touching the keyboard, then work through the numbered steps of the **Manoeuvres** on the computer. Complete the **S.A.E.** (Self-Assessment Exercise) at the end of the section to test your knowledge.

Driving Lesson 54 - Creating a New Template

Park and Read

A template can be based on an existing document <u>or</u> template. After changes have been made it can be saved in its own right as a new template.

Manoeuvres

1. Open the document **CV**.

2. Apply a 1pt black page border (**Format | Borders and Shading** and the **Page Border** tab) and delete the information at the right (all of the personal information).

3. To create the template, select **File | Save As**. Change the **File name** to **CV template** and **Save as type** to **Document Template**.

4. Notice how **Save in** automatically shows the **Templates** folder.

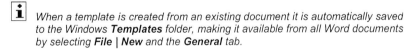

*When a template is created from an existing document it is automatically saved to the Windows **Templates** folder, making it available from all Word documents by selecting **File | New** and the **General** tab.*

5. Click **Save** and then close the template.

*To create a new template from an existing Word template, select **File | New**. From the **New** dialog box, choose the desired template and ensure **Template** is selected from **Create New**. Click **OK**.*

Driving Lesson 55 - Modifying a Template

Park and Read

It is possible to change a template as desired after it has been created, in the same way as normal documents can be edited.

Manoeuvres

1. Select **File | Open** and from **Look in** locate the **Templates** folder. Normally it can be found in **C:\Windows\Application Data\Microsoft**, but if you are on a network and cannot see it, check where templates are stored on your computer.

2. To apply a watermark, view the **Header and Footer**.

3. Insert a graphic of your choice from the **Business** category of the **Insert Clip Art** dialog box.

4. Close the **Header and Footer**.

5. Select all of the text in the document.

6. Change the font to **Book Antiqua**, or an alternative if this font is unavailable.

7. Save the template with the same name to overwrite the original. The changes are saved in the same way as a normal *Word* document, to the **Templates** folder.

8. Close the template.

9. Select **File | New** and the **General** tab. The **CV template** appears as an icon, ⊞ cvtemplate .

10. Don't open the template. It is to be deleted so that this Driving Lesson can be repeated on the same computer.

11. Right click on the **CV template** icon. Select **Delete** from the menu.

12. Select **Yes** at the prompt and click **Cancel** to close the dialog box.

Driving Lesson 56 - S.A.E.

This is a Self-Assessment Exercise, covering creating and modifying templates. Try to complete it without any reference to the previous Driving Lessons in this section.

1. Create a new template based on the **Elegant Letter** template.

2. Type your home address in the top text frame.

3. Change the font of all text to **Arial 11pt**.

4. Insert a graphic from the **Business** section as a watermark.

5. Tone down the graphic by right clicking and selecting **Format Picture**.

6. From the **Picture** tab's **Image control** area, click on the **Color** drop down list and select **Watermark**.

7. Click **OK** and close the **Header and Footer** dialog box.

8. Save the new template as **Business letter**.

9. Close the template.

10. Delete the template from the **New** dialog box.

If you experienced any difficulty completing this S.A.E. refer back to the Driving Lessons in this section. Then redo the S.A.E.

Once you are confident with the features, complete the Record of Achievement Matrix referring to the section at the end of the guide. Only when competent move on to the next Section.

Section 10
Collaborative Editing

By the end of this Section you should be able to:

Add and Remove Comments

Edit Comments

Track Changes to a Document

Accept or Reject Changes

To gain an understanding of the above features, work through the **Driving Lessons** in this **Section**.

For each **Driving Lesson**, read the **Park and Read** instructions, without touching the keyboard, then work through the numbered steps of the **Manoeuvres** on the computer. Complete the **S.A.E.** (Self-Assessment Exercise) at the end of the section to test your knowledge.

Driving Lesson 57 - Adding/Editing Comments

Park and Read

Comments are used to make notes on a document. They are usually for on-screen reference but can be printed if required.

Manoeuvres

1. Open **Shark**.

2. In the first paragraph highlight the word **Mediterranean**.

3. Select **Insert | Comment**. Mediterranean now has a coloured highlight.

4. In the **Comments** pane at the bottom of the screen, enter **It has recently been discovered that the Great White Shark comes here to breed.** Click **Close**.

5. **Mediterranean** appears highlighted. Select **Show/Hide, [¶]** and initials will appear along with the comment number.

[i] *They are the initials of the person who inserted the comment. The initials can be changed using* **Tools | Options | User Information**.

6. Find **cut** in the second paragraph and highlight it.

7. Select **Insert | Comment** and type **These cuts can result in shark attack**. Click **Close**.

8. Position the cursor over the word **Mediterranean** in the first paragraph. After a few seconds the comment appears, with the name of the person who created the comment.

9. Right click on the comment. Select **Edit Comment** from the shortcut menu.

10. The **Comments** pane appears. Edit the comment to **The Great White Shark uses the area as a nursery**.

11. Click **Close**.

12. Right click over the **cut** comment.

13. Select **Delete Comment** from the shortcut menu to delete the comment.

14. Save the document as **Comments**.

15. Close the document.

Driving Lesson 58 - Tracking Changes

▣ Park and Read

By tracking changes to a document, it is possible to see where, when and who made the changes to it. Text that has been added to and deleted from a document is shown.

☞ Manoeuvres

1. Open **CiA**. This is a draft version of the document.

2. Select **Tools | Track Changes | Highlight Changes**. Check **Track changes while editing**.

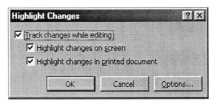

ℹ️ *To turn tracking off, uncheck **Track changes while editing***

3. Click **OK**.

4. At the end of the first paragraph, enter **Although the company is based in the North East, training can be provided throughout the country**.

5. Notice that the words have been coloured. This denotes that the text has been added to the document.

6. Delete **usually at no extra cost** on the last line of the third paragraph. The text appears as strikethrough to show it has been deleted.

7. Go to the end of the document.

8. Start a new paragraph and enter the following text: **For more information ring 0191 549 5002**.

9. Notice how the amended areas are noted in the left margin.

10. Save the document as **Tracking** but do not close it.

ℹ️ *Changes to tracking marks can be made from **Options** in the **Highlight Changes** dialog box.*

Driving Lesson 59 - Accepting and Rejecting Changes

◪ Park and Read

Once changes have been tracked in a document, it is possible to view each change and accept it or reject it. This is very useful when creating a joint report, or similar document.

Manoeuvres

1. Use **Tracking** for this lesson and move to the top of the document.

2. Select **Tools | Track Changes | Accept or Reject Changes** to display the following dialog box.

3. Click on [➡ Find] to move to the first change. Notice how the **Changes** area states what has been changed and by whom.

4. To accept the change, i.e. accept the added text, click on [Accept].

5. The next change is highlighted. Accept this change.

6. Reject the last change.

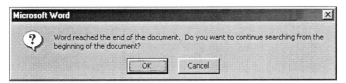

7. Click **Cancel** in the dialog box that appears, then **Close** the **Accept or Reject Changes** dialog box.

8. Notice that no text is now highlighted. This is because the changes have been either accepted or rejected.

9. Select **Tools | Track Changes | Highlight Changes** and uncheck **Track changes while editing** to edit text normally. Confirm this by clicking **OK**.

10. Save the document as **Final** before closing it.

Driving Lesson 60 - S.A.E.

This is a Self-Assessment Exercise, covering comments, tracking changes and accepting or rejecting changes. Try to complete it without any reference to the previous Driving Lessons in this section.

1.　Open the document **Colorado**.

2.　Set it up to track changes.

3.　Insert a bold, centred **16pt** heading: **Colorado**.

4.　Change the font size of the remainder of the text to **12pt**.

5.　Make the first paragraph italic.

6.　At the end of the final paragraph, enter **This natural wonder attracts hundreds of thousands of tourists annually.**

7.　In the final paragraph, enter a **comment** after **marine sediment**, with the text **many fossils of sea creatures have been found.**

8.　Work through the changes, accepting all apart from the inserted text, which should be rejected.

9.　Close the document <u>without</u> saving.

If you experienced any difficulty completing this S.A.E. refer back to the Driving Lessons in this section. Then redo the S.A.E.

Once you are confident with the features, complete the Record of Achievement Matrix referring to the section at the end of the guide. Only when competent move on to the next Section.

Section 11
Document Security

By the end of this Section you should be able to:

Password Protect a Document

Change Passwords

Remove Password Protection

To gain an understanding of the above features, work through the **Driving Lessons** in this **Section**.

For each **Driving Lesson**, read the **Park and Read** instructions, without touching the keyboard, then work through the numbered steps of the **Manoeuvres** on the computer. Complete the **S.A.E.** (Self-Assessment Exercise) at the end of the section to test your knowledge.

Driving Lesson 61 - Password Protection

🄿 Park and Read

If a computer is shared a password can be assigned to certain documents to restrict access to them. Passwords can be set to allow a document be opened or modified only. Be careful, as without the password access to the document will not be allowed; make sure to use a password that will not be forgotten.

⌐ Manoeuvres

1. Open the document **Minutes**.

2. To add a password of your choice select **File | Save As | Tools | General Options**.

i *Passwords can also be entered by selecting* ***Tools | Options | Save****.*

3. From the **Save** tab, locate **File sharing options for "Minutes"** and enter your password in **Password to open**.

i *Passwords are case sensitive, therefore Samantha is not the same as samantha or SAMANTHA.*

4. Select **OK**. Re-enter the same password in the **Re-enter password to open** box, click **OK** and save the document as **Password**.

5. Close the document.

6. To check whether it worked, open the document **Password**, using your password when prompted.

7. Leave the document open for the next lesson.

Driving Lesson 62 - Removing and Changing Passwords

Park and Read

If it is decided to change or remove a password, follow the same general steps as for adding a password. The document must be saved after the password is changed.

Manoeuvres

1. Use the document **Password**.

2. A rumour is circulating that the canteen workers have accessed the document. For security reasons, change to a different password using **File | Save As | Tools | General Options**.

> **i** *Password options are also available from **Tools | Options | Save**.*

3. In the **Password to open** area, enter a new password and click **OK**. Re-enter the password and click **OK**.

4. Save and then close the document.

5. Scandal is imminent - the document has been released to the press. Reopen the document and remove the password by deleting the contents in the **Password to open** box. Click **OK**.

6. Save the document and close it.

7. Check that the document is no longer password protected by reopening it.

8. Close the document.

> **i** *Passwords can only be changed when the document is open and can only be opened with the password. Therefore, passwords cannot be accidentally changed.*

Driving Lesson 63 - S.A.E.

This is a Self-Assessment Exercise, covering adding, changing and removing passwords. Try to complete it without any reference to the previous Driving Lessons in this section.

1.   Open the document **Articles**.

2.   Save the document as **Top Secret**.

3.   Apply a password to open it.

4.   Test the password.

5.   Change the password to **Secret**.

6.   Test the password again.

7.   Remove the password protection.

8.   Save the document using the same filename.

9.   Close the document.

If you experienced any difficulty completing this S.A.E. refer back to the Driving Lessons in this section. Then redo the S.A.E.

Once you are confident with the features, complete the Record of Achievement Matrix referring to the section at the end of the guide. Only when competent move on to the next Section.

Section 12
Master Documents

By the end of this Section you should be able to:

Create a Master Document

Create a Subdocument

Add or Remove a Subdocument

To gain an understanding of the above features, work through the **Driving Lessons** in this **Section**.

For each **Driving Lesson**, read the **Park and Read** instructions, without touching the keyboard, then work through the numbered steps of the **Manoeuvres** on the computer. Complete the **S.A.E.** (Self-Assessment Exercise) at the end of the section to test your knowledge.

Driving Lesson 64 - Creating a Master Document

▣ Park and Read

A **Master Document** is used when a report is too long to be maintained as one document. **Subdocuments** can be created, then inserted into the Master Document. They can be printed individually or altogether. They can also be used to create Tables of Contents. Master Documents can be used in **Outline** view to organise headings, contents and indexes.

☞ Manoeuvres

1. Start a new document and switch to **Outline** view.

2. Click **Master Document View** to display all buttons.

3. Notice the **Master Document** buttons at the right of the **Outlining** toolbar.

4. With the style as **Heading 1**, enter the title **The Book I Always Wanted to Write**.

5. Press <**Enter**>.

6. Change the style of the next line to **Heading 2**.

7. Type in the text **Chapter One**. The **Master Document** is now ready to have subdocuments added.

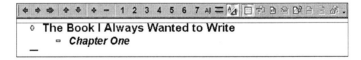

8. Leave the document open and move to the next Driving Lesson.

Driving Lesson 65 - Creating a Sub-Document

▣ Park and Read

A **Subdocument** is created and saved in the same way as a normal document. Once a subdocument is inserted/created in a **Master Document**, the two documents are linked. This allows the subdocument to be opened and changed individually, or through the Master Document. A Master Document can also help members of a workgroup to create and update parts of a long document.

Manoeuvres

1. With the insertion point still at the end of the chapter one text, select **Create Subdocument** ⊞. This places the chapter heading inside a grey outline, defining the subdocument.

2. Save the document as **My Book**. The subdocument will automatically be saved as **Chapter One**.

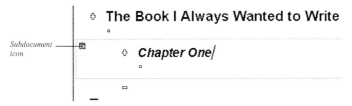

3. Double click on the subdocument icon to open **Chapter One**. Underneath the title (using the **Normal** style) enter **I was born in the early summer of 19##**. Click on **Save**.

4. Using the **Taskbar**, switch back to **My Book** to view the reflected changes. Close both documents, saving if prompted.

5. Open **My Book**. Note how the subdocument is now displayed only as a file name A:\Chapter One.doc. Move the pointer over the file name until it changes to a hand. Click once on the file name to open the document.

6. Close it again. Click at the end of the **Chapter One** file name, taking care not to click when the hand is in view. Click on **Expand Subdocuments** ⊞. All of the entered text is now displayed. Text can also be entered here.

Driving Lesson 65 - Continued

7. Click beside the last text entry icon ▫ and enter **Chapter Two**. Make this a subdocument by clicking on 🗎. Save **My Book**.

8. Double click on **Chapter Two**'s subdocument icon and enter the text **I went to school at....** Close and save **Chapter Two**.

9. Collapse the subdocuments using 🔁. The **Master Document** appears as below.

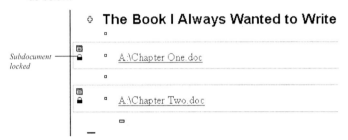

10. Subdocuments are usually **locked** when they are not to be modified, i.e. are read-only. However, in this case, expand the documents and the locks will be opened.

11. Click on **Master Document** 🔲 to view where the **Section Breaks** (dotted lines) occur. Note that they are before and after each subdocument. Section Breaks were covered in a previous Driving Lesson.

12. Click on 🔲 again and collapse the subdocuments. **Print Preview** the **Master Document** selecting **Yes** at the dialog box.

13. Close **Print Preview**, but leave **My Book** open.

Driving Lesson 66 - Adding and Removing a Sub-Document

▣ Park and Read

Previously created documents can be used as subdocuments.

⌒ Manoeuvres

1. Use the Master Document **My Book**, which should still be open from the previous Driving Lesson.

2. Click beside the last text entry icon ▭ and click the **Insert Subdocument** button, 🗒.

3. From the data files, select the document **Chapter 3** and click **Open**.

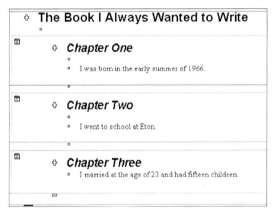

4. The document is inserted as a subdocument.

5. To delete the **Chapter 3** subdocument, first make sure the subdocuments are expanded.

6. Click on the **Chapter 3** subdocument icon and press <**Delete**> to remove it.

7. Save and close **My Book**.

Driving Lesson 67 - S.A.E.

This is a Self-Assessment Exercise, covering creating a master document, adding and removing subdocuments. Try to complete it without any reference to the previous Driving Lessons in this section.

1. Create a master document from the following files: **Beverages, Cuisine** and **Deli**.

2. Save the master document as **Food and drink**.

3. Preview the master document then adjust the section breaks so that there are only three pages (you may need to switch views to do this).

4. Remove the subdocument **Deli**.

5. Save the changes to the master document.

6. Close it.

If you experienced any difficulty completing this S.A.E. refer back to the Driving Lessons in this section. Then redo the S.A.E.

Once you are confident with the features, complete the Record of Achievement Matrix referring to the section at the end of the guide. Only when competent move on to the next Section.

Section 13
Field Codes and
Forms

By the end of this Section you should be able to:

Insert, Delete, Edit and Update Field Codes

Field Codes

Lock or Unlock a Field

Create and Edit a Form

Change Form Field Options

Protect and Delete Form Fields

To gain an understanding of the above features, work through the **Driving Lessons** in this **Section**.

For each **Driving Lesson**, read the **Park and Read** instructions, without touching the keyboard, then work through the numbered steps of the **Manoeuvres** on the computer. Complete the **S.A.E.** (Self-Assessment Exercise) at the end of the section to test your knowledge.

Driving Lesson 68 - Working With Field Codes

▣ Park and Read

Fields are used to insert codes, which are updated to print current information, e.g. indexes, dates, etc. Fields can also be used as a basis for a set document, where fields are given descriptive names and are then replaced with the appropriate text.

☞ Manoeuvres

1. This lesson demonstrates the use of fields in a document header. Open the document **Summary**.

2. Select **File | Properties** and add your name to the document as **Author** and **Minutes** as the **Title**. Click **OK**.

3. Select **View | Header and Footer**. The **Header** appears, together with the **Header and Footer** toolbar.

4. In the **Header** (with the cursor at the left margin), select **Insert | Field**.

5. From the **Categories**, select **Document Information** and then select **Author** from **Field names**. Click **OK**.

6. Tab to the centre. The **Header and Footer** toolbar can be used to add the name of the document as a code. Select **Insert | AutoText** and choose **Filename** from the list.

7. Click the **Switch between Header and Footer** button, ▣.

8. At the left of the **Footer**, insert the time by clicking the **Insert Time** button, ▣.

9. Tab to the right of the **Footer** and click the **Insert Date** button, ▣, to insert the current date as a field.

10. Close the **Footer** using the **Close** button, or by double clicking on a blank area of the screen. Print a copy of the document.

11. Save the document as **Fields** and close it.

12. Open **CiA**. Add the **Date**, **Time** and **Filename** to the **Footer**.

13. Print a copy of the document and close it <u>without</u> saving.

14. Open **Fields** and print the document again. Look at the time in the **Footer**. It shows the time the document was printed.

15. Close the document <u>without</u> saving.

Driving Lesson 69 - Editing and Updating Field Codes

◪ Park and Read

Fields containing information that changes, for example the time, can be updated to give new results by using the <F9> function key. Most fields are updated indirectly when printing or merging.

☞ Manoeuvres

1. Open the document **Interview**. From **Tools | Options, View** tab, ensure **Field codes** is checked, to view the fields that are in the document.

2. To move to the first field code and replace the contents, press <**F11**>. The cursor moves into the first field, which is **{Date}**. Select **Insert | Date and Time**, choose an appropriate format, then click **OK**. Press <**F11**> to move to the next field, **{Name}**.

3. Type **Mr Barker** to replace the field. Press <**F11**> to move to the next field and enter **Dog Handler**.

ⓘ *Use <F11> or <Alt F1> to move from field to field. To move backwards, use <Shift F11>.*

4. Move to the next field and enter the interview date as next **Tuesday**.

5. In the next field, enter **2pm** for the time. Enter **references** in the next field.

6. Print a copy of the letter.

7. To delete the date field, highlight the **{Date}** field code and press the **<Delete>** key.

8. Close the document <u>without</u> saving.

ⓘ *To switch between viewing field codes and field results either select **Tools | Options | View | Field codes** or <Alt F9>.*

9. Open the document **Time**. Make sure **Field codes** is checked and press <**Alt F9**> to view the actual times.

10. To update a single field, the cursor must be within the field. Position the cursor inside the **1:39:20** in the first line. Press <**F9**> to update the time.

11. Try this again using the time on the second line.

ⓘ *To make sure that all fields are updated when printed, select **Tools | Options | Print** and check the **Update fields** box.*

12. Leave the document open for the next Driving Lesson.

Driving Lesson 70 - Locking/Unlocking Fields

▣ Park and Read

Sometimes fields may not require updating. In order to keep a specific result, the **Lock Field** key <Ctrl F11> is used.

☞ Manoeuvres

1. Use the document **Time** for this Driving Lesson.

2. Try updating the time on the third line. This time has been locked; the time is fixed and will not be updated.

[i] *To unlock a locked field press <**Ctrl Shift F11**> the **Unlock Field** key.*

3. Highlight the time in line 4. Lock the field by pressing **<Ctrl F11>**.

4. Try updating the field using **<F9>**.

5. Now unlock the field by pressing **<Ctrl Shift F11>**. Use **<F9>** to update.

6. Close the document without saving.

Driving Lesson 71 - Creating and Editing Forms

Park and Read

Form Fields are created to speed up the completion of forms. The layout of the form is designed first, then the fields are created.

The form must be protected before the fields will work.

Manoeuvres

1. Start a new document and enter the text as below:

    Memo

    To:

    From:

    Date:

    Subject:

    Urgent:

    Message:

2. Select all of the text and insert a left tab stop at **3cm**.

3. Position the cursor after **To:** and press <Tab> to move to the tab stop.

4. Select **View | Toolbars | Forms** to view the **Forms** toolbar.

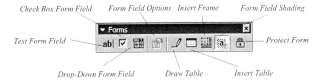

Check Box Form Field *Form Field Options* *Insert Frame* *Form Field Shading*

Text Form Field *Protect Form*

Drop-Down Form Field *Draw Table* *Insert Table*

5. Click once on **Drop-Down Form Field**, to create a field.

6. To delete the field, place the cursor in front of it and press <Delete> once to highlight the field, then again to delete it.

7. Now create the **Drop-Down Form Field** again, as it is needed for this form.

8. Leave the document open for the next Driving Lesson.

Driving Lesson 72 - Form Field Options

▣ Park and Read

After a form field has been created, the choices given within the field have to be set, using form field options.

☞ Manoeuvres

1. Using the document from the previous Driving Lesson, keep the cursor in the field and press the **Form Field Options** button, ▣.

2. In **Drop-down item**, enter **Andrew Simpson**. Click on **Add**.

3. Enter the following names in the same manner: **Susan Peters, Ishmael Rampuri** and **Gita Patel**. Click **OK** to close the dialog box.

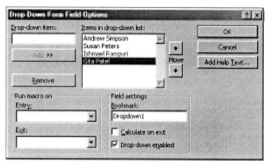

4. Click after **From** and press **<Tab>**. Click on the **Text Form Field** button, abl, to create a field. Click ▣ to display the options for the field and in **Default text**, enter your name and click **OK**.

5. Create a **Text Form Field** after **Date**. Click ▣ to define options for this field.

6. From **Type**, select **Current date** and in the **Date format** box, select **dd MMMM yyyy**. Click **OK**.

7. Place a **Text Form Field** after **Subject**. Click after **Urgent**, press **<Tab>**, then click on the **Check Box Form Field** button, ☑.

8. Finally, create a **Text Form Field** on the line below **Message**.

9. Leave the document open for the next Driving Lesson.

Driving Lesson 73 - Protecting Form Fields

Park and Read

To allow the fields to work a document must be protected.

Manoeuvres

1. Using the document from the previous Driving Lesson, click the **Protect Form** button, 🔒.

2. Save the document as **Form**.

3. Click in the first field - a drop down arrow appears.

4. Choose a name, then press <**Tab**> to move to the next field.

5. Press <**Tab**> again to move to the **Subject**. Notice that the date is automatically set as the current date.

6. In **Subject**, enter **Important Notice** and click once in the field box next to **Urgent**.

7. Press <**Tab**> and enter the following message:

    Please note that the budget has been cut by 10%, therefore I will need new costings urgently.

8. Print the document, then save it as **Form2**.

9. Close the document.

Driving Lesson 74 - S.A.E.

This is a Self-Assessment Exercise, covering forms and form fields. Try to complete it without any reference to the previous Driving Lessons in this section.

1. Open the document **Interview** and use the fields to make the following amendments: invite **Ms Walker** to an interview for the position of **Mountain Rescue Officer** next **Thursday** at **10am**. She must bring **outward bound certificates** with her.

2. Print the document.

3. Close it <u>without</u> saving and open **Reservation**.

4. Leave a space after the address and insert a date field.

5. At the bottom of the letter, type **Letter created at** and insert a time field.

6. Print the document.

7. Change the **Author** details to your name.

8. Update the time field and close the document <u>without</u> saving.

9. Start a new document to create a form inviting four colleagues to a meeting. Enter the text as below:

   Meeting Schedule
   To:
   From:
   Date:
   Time:
   Agenda:
   Reply req?

10. Set a tab at **4cm** for all of the text, then click after **To:** and press <Tab>. Insert a **Drop-Down Form Field** and enter the names of four colleagues (don't forget to use the **Form Field Options**).

11. Create **Text Form Fields** for **From: Date: Time:** and **Agenda:**.

12. Create a **Check Box Form Field** after **Reply req?** and **Protect** the form.

13. Select a name from the list for **To:**, enter your name in **From:**, enter today's date and the time as the current time. Check the check box.

14. Save the document as **Meeting** and close it. Close the **Forms** toolbar.

If you experienced any difficulty completing this S.A.E. refer back to the Driving Lessons in this section. Then redo the S.A.E.

Once you are confident with the features, complete the Record of Achievement Matrix referring to the section at the end of the guide. Only when competent move on to the next Section.

Section 14
Mail Merge

By the end of this Section you should be able to:

Edit a Mail Merge Data Source

Sort and Query a Data Source

Use Different Data Sources

To gain an understanding of the above features, work through the **Driving Lessons** in this **Section**.

For each **Driving Lesson**, read the **Park and Read** instructions, without touching the keyboard, then work through the numbered steps of the **Manoeuvres** on the computer. Complete the **S.A.E.** (Self-Assessment Exercise) at the end of the section to test your knowledge.

Driving Lesson 75 - Editing a Data Source

▣ Park and Read

A **Data Source** can be used with any number of **Main Documents**, so it must be well planned. However, the data source may have to be edited, for example if someone on a mailing list changes his or her address.

Manoeuvres

1. Open the document **Clients**. This is a mail merge data source and can be edited in the same way as other documents.

2. Freda Jones, the first person on the list, has left the country. Select the entire row containing her record. To remove the record, select **Table | Delete | Rows**.

3. BB Computer Consultants have moved to 49 George Street. Amend the record accordingly.

4. Close the data source without saving.

5. Now open the document **Invitation**. It is also possible to edit a data source from within a main document using the **Mail Merge Helper**.

6. Click the **Mail Merge Helper** button, [⊞] and from section **2**, click on **Edit**, then on **Clients** from the list (the **Edit Data Source** button, [⊞], can also be used to edit from within the main document).

7. George Murphy has asked to be removed from the mailing list. His record is number **2**. View the record on the **Data Form**, click the **Delete** button.

8. Now click **View Source** to see the data source file. Notice that George Murphy's record has been removed.

9. Leave the **Clients** and **Invitation** documents open for the next Driving Lesson.

Driving Lesson 76 - Sorting a Data Source

Park and Read

It is possible to sort the records in a data source in ascending or descending alphabetical or numerical order. A data source can also be queried, to send letters only to people in a particular city, for example.

Manoeuvres

1. Using the data source **Clients**, make sure the **Database** toolbar is showing (**View | Toolbars | Database**).

2. To sort the data alphabetically by company, place the cursor in the **Company** row.

3. Click the **Sort Ascending** button, on the **Database** toolbar.

4. Notice how the records are now sorted in ascending alphabetical order.

Name	Company	Street	Town	Region
Alison Biggs	A.B. Dental Studios	Mile End Road	Oswestry	Shropshire
Ann George	Acorn Alarms	7 Tadcaster Road	Sunderland	Tyne and Wear
Jean Chadwick	B&J Industrial Services	54 High Close	Oldham	Lancs
Freda Jones	B.O. Designs	45 Cloth Market	Newcastle Under Lyme	Staffs
Brian Bigg	BB Computer Consultants	28 George Street	Sunderland	Tyne and Wear
Sharon Walls	Butterfly Engineering	Central Buildings	Ludlow	Shropshire
Jez Carter	Carters' Gold Dealers	Argyll Street	Spalding	Lincs
Ian Chaplin	Chaplins Wine	The Barn	Sunderland	Tyne and Wear
Aaron Dowson	Direct Pickles	66 Bright Street	Luton	Beds
Brian Wood	Floral Designs	136 New Street	Georgetown	London
Ian Smith	Glasgow Potato Company	The Dell	South Shields	Tyne and Wear
Keith Summers	H.T. Bank	Riverside House	Swavesey	Cambs
Karen Jones	Hair Care	130 Park Road	Ilminster	Somerset
David Jay	Jays Birds	56 Blackbird Way	Dorchester	Dorset
Ian Charteris	Manor House Hotel	Dreghorn Road	Clonmel	Waterford
Tony Charterhouse	Modular Shelving	38 The Oaks	Billingshurst	West Sussex
Steve Chapman	Phoenix Glass	Darlington Road	Reading	Berkshire
Ros Smithson	Pipe	88 North Avenue	Sunderland	Tyne and Wear
Charles Houghton	Pretty Ceramics	Unit 11 Arms Ind Estate	Sunderland	Tyne and Wear
Eileen Smithers	Radiophone	10 South Street	Hetton	Norwich
Philip Orwell	Russell Hotel	Edinburgh Road	Paisley	Renfrewshire
Tracy Talbot	Shortcut Hairdressers	Adlington Road	Stockport	Cheshire
Janet Perfect	Station Taxis	111 Station Road	Newcastle upon Tyne	Tyne and Wear
Eileen Murphy	The Decorative Co.	743 Yarm Road	Yarm	Cleveland
Eileen Charterhouse	The Deli	99 Sea Road	Bridlington	Yorks
Margaret Fenwick	The Outdoor Centre	34 The Oaks	Billingshurst	West Sussex
Karen Armstrong	Turner Plant Hire	Unit 2D	Liverpool	Merseyside
George Murphy	Unique Bathrooms Ltd	Bridge Street	Alton	Hampshire
Billy Wonder	Waltons Ltd	Bywell Industrial Estate	High Wycombe	Bucks
Jim Burroughs	Wonder Plastercrafts	15 Priest Close	Springwell	Derby
Des Young	Wynward Garage	Main Road	Clwyd	North Wales
	Youngs Aquatics	27 South View	Poole	Dorset

5. To sort the records in descending alphabetical order, make sure the cursor is still in the **Company** row.

6. Click the **Sort Descending** button, .

Driving Lesson 76 - Continued

Name	Company	Street	Town	Region
Des Young	Youngs Aquatics	27 South View	Poole	Dorset
Jim Burroughs	Wynward Garage	Main Road	Clwyd	North Wales
Billy Wonder	Wonder Plastercrafts	15 Priest Close	Springwell	Derby
George Murphy	Waltons Ltd	Bywell Industrial Estate	High Wycombe	Bucks
Karen Armstrong	Unique Bathrooms Ltd	Bridge Street	Alton	Hampshire
Margaret Fenwick	Turner Plant Hire	Unit 2D	Liverpool	Merseyside
Eileen Charterhouse	The Outdoor Centre	34 The Oaks	Billinghurst	West Sussex
Eileen Murphy	The Deli	99 Sea Road	Bridlington	Yorks
Janet Perfect	The Decorative Co.	743 Yarm Road	Yarm	Cleveland
Tracy Talbot	Station Taxis	111 Station Road	Newcastle upon Tyne	Tyne and Wear
Philip Orwell	Shorton Hairdressers	Adlington Road	Stockport	Cheshire
Ishmail Rampuri	Russell Hotel	Edinburgh Road	Paisley	Renfrewshire
Eileen Smithers	Radiophone	10 South Street	Hetton	Norwich
Charles Houghton	Pretty Ceramics	Unit 11 Atms Ind Estate	Sunderland	Tyne and Wear
Ros Smithson	Pips	88 North Avenue	Sunderland	Tyne and Wear
Steve Chapman	Phoenix Glass	Darlington Road	Reading	Berkshire
Tony Charterhouse	Modular Shelving	38 The Oaks	Billinghurst	West Sussex
Ian Charteris	Manor House Hotel	Dreghorn Road	Clonmel	Waterford
David Jay	Jays Birds	56 Blackbird Way	Dorchester	Dorset
Karen Jones	Hair Care	130 Park Road	Ilminster	Somerset
Keith Summers	H.T. Bank	Riverside House	Swavesey	Cambs
Ian Smith	Glasgow Potato Company	The Dell	South Shields	Tyne and Wear
Brian Wood	Floral Designs	136 New Street	Georgetown	London
Aaron Dowson	Direct Pickles	66 Bright Street	Luton	Beds
Ian Chaplin	Chaplins Wine	The Barn	Sunderland	Tyne and Wear
Jez Carter	Carters' Gold Dealers	Argyll Street	Spalding	Lincs
Sharon Walls	Butterfly Engineering	Central Buildings	Ludlow	Shropshire
Brian Bigg	BE Computer Consultants	28 George Street	Sunderland	Tyne and Wear
Freda Jones	B.G. Designs	45 Cloth Market	Newcastle Under Lyme	Staffs
Jean Chadwick	B&J Industrial Services	34 High Close	Oldham	Lancs
Ann George	Acorn Alarms	7 Tadcaster Road	Sunderland	Tyne and Wear
Alison Biggs	A.B. Dental Studios	Mile End Road	Oswestry	Shropshire

7. To query this data source and send letters to people living in **Tyne and Wear**, but not to the others, click **Mail Merge Helper**, ▦.

8. From part **3** click **Query Options** and complete the dialog box as below:

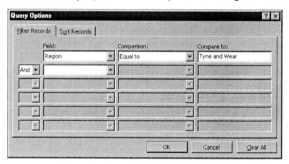

9. Click **OK**.

10. From part **3** of the **Mail Merge Helper**, click **Merge** and make sure **Merge to** shows **New document**.

11. Click **Merge**. There should be 7 letters. Check the addresses, which should all be in **Tyne and Wear**.

12. Close **Form Letters1** and **Clients** without saving the changes.

13. Leave **Invitation** open.

Driving Lesson 77 - Using Various Data Sources

Park and Read

When performing mail merge, you are not restricted to using data sources created in *Word*. It is also possible to use a table from an *Access* database, for example.

Manoeuvres

1. Use the main document **Invitation** for this Driving Lesson. Your colleague in Marketing has given you a database containing 10 new customers, to whom you want to send an invitation to the company's open day.

2. Click the **Mail Merger Helper**, then click **Get Data**.

3. From the drop down list, select **Open Data Source**.

4. Make sure **Files of type** at the bottom of the dialog box shows **MS Access Databases** and **Look in** shows the location of the data files.

5. Select the **Contacts** database and click **Open**.

6. The **Contact List** table should be selected in the **Microsoft Access** dialog box. Click **OK**.

7. Now the main document has to be edited to contain the correct merge fields. Click on **Edit** from section **1** of the **Mail Merge Helper** and select **Invitation**.

Driving Lesson 77 - Continued

8. Delete the existing merge fields in the document.

9. Click on the **Insert Merge Field** button to reveal the list of available fields in the *Access* table.

10. Place the new fields in the main document so that they match the diagram below.

11. Click 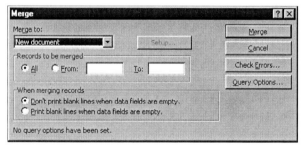 again, then select **Merge** and **Merge** again, making sure **New document** is selected from **Merge to**.

12. Print preview the merge document, which should contain 10 letters.

13. Close all documents <u>without</u> saving.

Driving Lesson 78 - S.A.E.

This is a Self-Assessment Exercise, covering editing and sorting a data source and using a different data source. Try to complete it without any reference to the previous Driving Lessons in this section.

1. Open the document **Conference**. This is a prepared mail merge letter.

2. Use the **Edit Data Source** button, [image], to view the data form.

3. Change Aaron Dowson's company name to **Pickles Direct**.

4. Click on **View Source**.

5. Sort the records by name, alphabetically.

6. Close all documents <u>without</u> saving.

7. Open **Conference** again.

8. To open a new data source – an *Access* database, select the **Conferences** database from the *Access* dialog box and the **No training** query.

9. Edit the main document, **Conference**, removing the original merge fields.

10. Insert the following fields in suitable positions:

    First Name

    Last Name

    Company

    Address1

    Address2

    City

11. Merge to a new document.

12. Print the merged document.

13. Close all documents <u>without</u> saving.

If you experienced any difficulty completing this S.A.E. refer back to the Driving Lessons in this section. Then redo the S.A.E.

Once you are confident with the features, complete the Record of Achievement Matrix referring to the section at the end of the guide. Only when competent move on to the next Section.

Section 15
Working with
Spreadsheets

By the end of this Section you should be able to:

Modify an Embedded Worksheet

Create a Chart from a Worksheet

Modify a Chart

To gain an understanding of the above features, work through the **Driving Lessons** in this **Section**.

For each **Driving Lesson**, read the **Park and Read** instructions, without touching the keyboard, then work through the numbered steps of the **Manoeuvres** on the computer. Complete the **S.A.E.** (Self-Assessment Exercise) at the end of the section to test your knowledge.

Driving Lesson 79 - Modifying a Worksheet

🄿 Park and Read

A worksheet can be created in *Excel* and then it can be inserted into *Word*. Changes to the worksheet can be made within *Word*.

Manoeuvres

1. Start a new document and change the orientation to **Landscape**.

2. Select **Insert | Object** and the **Create from File** tab.

3. Browse for **Sales** from the data files. This is an *Excel* file.

4. Select it and click **Insert**.

5. In the **Object** dialog box, click on **OK**.

6. Double click on the embedded worksheet and if necessary, resize it until all of the data can be seen.

7. Click in cell **D6** and change the figure for **Central**'s **June** sales to **£150,000**.

8. Press **<Enter>**.

	A	B	C	D	E	F
1						
2		Company Sales				
3						
4			*North*	*Central*	*South*	
5		*May*	£130,000	£110,743	£90,466	
6		*June*	£140,376	£150,000	£100,744	
7		*July*	£140,244	£120,500	£140,775	
8						
9						
10						
11						
12						
13						
14						
15						

Chart \ Sales

9. Save the document as **Central Sales**.

10. Leave the document open for the next **Driving Lesson**.

Driving Lesson 80 - Creating a Chart

▣ Park and Read

A chart can be created from an *Excel* worksheet that has been pasted or embedded into a document. A chart can also be created from a *Word* table.

⌐ Manoeuvres

1. Use **Central Sales** for this Driving Lesson.

2. Make sure the worksheet is selected (has handles) and click and drag to select from cell **B4** to **E7**.

3. Click the **Chart Wizard** button,

4. From the list of chart types, select **Bar** and leave the **sub-type** as a **Clustered Bar**.

5. Click **Next** and then **Next** again.

6. At step **3** enter the **Chart title** as **Company Sales**, the **Category (x) axis** as **Region** and the **Value (y) axis** as **Sales**.

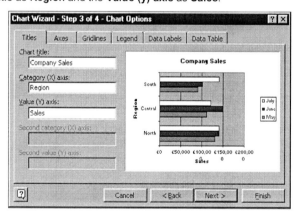

Driving Lesson 80 - Continued

7. Click **Next** and choose to place the chart **As object in Sales**.

8. Click **Finish** to place the chart on the worksheet. Notice that the **Chart** toolbar has appeared (if not, select **View | Toolbars | Chart**).

9. Resize the worksheet until there is enough room to move the chart beneath it by dragging the bottom middle handle down.

10. Move the mouse pointer over the bottom border of the chart until it becomes a north-west pointing arrow.

11. Click and drag the chart beneath the worksheet. If necessary enlarge it so that all **Regions** can be seen.

12. Leave **Central Sales** open and start a new document, to create a chart from a table.

13. Type the heading **Average Temperatures 2001** and insert a **4x4** table. Complete the table as below:

Average Temperatures 2001

	Paris	Madrid	Rome
June	23	28	27
July	28	30	31
August	29	32	33

14. Select the table and then **Insert | Picture | Chart**. If necessary use the **Title Bar** of the datasheet to click and drag it out of the way, so the chart can be seen.

15. On the datasheet, change **Madrid's August** temperature to **35**.

16. Notice how the chart reflects the change, but the original table does <u>not</u>. Likewise, changes made to the table will not be shown in the chart. This is different from an embedded *Excel* worksheet, where changes made to the original data are shown in the chart.

17. Close this document <u>without</u> saving, but leave **Central Sales** open for the next Driving Lesson.

Driving Lesson 81 - Modifying a Chart

▣ Park and Read

Once a chart has been created, it can be edited at any time. Editing must be performed in **Datasheet View**. It is also possible to format any area of a chart by double clicking on it and selecting from the available options.

☞ Manoeuvres

1. The chart created in the previous Driving Lesson should still be open. Make sure it is selected.

2. Click in cell **C5** and change the sales figure to **£80,000**.

3. Notice how the chart changes to reflect the new figure.

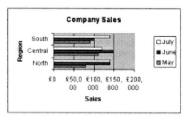

4. Move the mouse over the grey **Plot Area** of the chart (a **ToolTip** will appear to confirm the pointer is in the right position).

5. Double click to open the **Format Plot Area** dialog box.

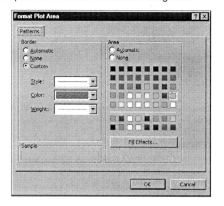

Driving Lesson 81 - Continued

6. From the **Border** area, click on the **Color** drop down list and select **Teal**.

7. From **Area** select **Aqua** and notice the **Sample** at the bottom left of the dialog box.

8. Click **OK** to apply the formatting.

9. Double click on the **Company Sales Chart Title**.

10. Select the **Font** tab from the **Format Chart Title** dialog box and choose the **Calisto MT** font (or an alternative).

11. Change the colour of the font to **Dark Blue** and click **OK**.

12. Now click on the **Series** for **June**. Double click on any one of the three squares that appear on each series.

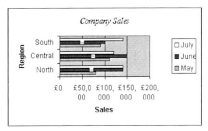

13. Change the **Area** colour to **Bright Green** and click **OK**.

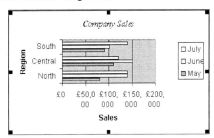

14. Save the changes to the document and close it.

Driving Lesson 82 - S.A.E.

This is a Self-Assessment Exercise, covering worksheets, inserting and modifying charts. Try to complete it without any reference to the previous Driving Lessons in this section.

1. Start a new document and insert the *Excel* worksheet **Toy sales**.

2. Change the **Teddy bear** sales to **75**.

3. Create a pie chart with the title **Toy Sales April 2001**.

4. Click on the **Data Labels** tab at step 3 of the **Wizard** and select the **Show percent** option. Create the chart as an object.

5. Change the sales of the **Spacehopper** to **85**.

6. Print the document.

7. Close it <u>without</u> saving.

If you experienced any difficulty completing this S.A.E. refer back to the Driving Lessons in this section. Then redo the S.A.E.

Once you are confident with the features, complete the Record of Achievement Matrix referring to the section at the end of the guide. Only when competent move on to the next Section.

Section 16
Macros

By the end of this Section you should be able to

Record a Macro

Run a Macro

Copy a Macro

Assign a Macro to a Button

To gain an understanding of the above features, work through the **Driving Lessons** in this **Section**.

For each **Driving Lesson**, read the **Park and Read** instructions, without touching the keyboard, then work through the numbered steps of the **Manoeuvres** on the computer. Complete the **S.A.E.** (Self-Assessment Exercise) at the end of the section to test your knowledge.

Driving Lesson 83 - Recording a Macro

▣ Park and Read

A **Macro** records keystrokes and menu selections, then plays them back exactly as they were recorded. A macro can be created so that a commonly used task can be performed, or a word, phrase or paragraph can be entered automatically. The use of macros results in the more efficient production of documents. Once macros have been created, they can be used at any time in any document that uses the same template.

A new macro can be created easily, but great care must be taken during the recording, because each action taken is incorporated into the macro.

⌐ Manoeuvres

1. Open a new document. A macro is to be created to complete a letter.

2. Select **Tools | Macro | Record New Macro**.

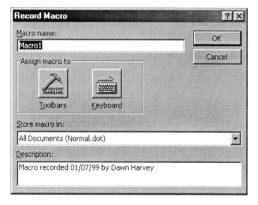

3. Enter the **Macro name** as **Signature** and in **Description**, enter **My signature** to replace the text.

4. Click **OK**. At this point the message **REC** is displayed in the **Status Bar** and the **Macro** toolbar is visible.

Driving Lesson 83 - Continued

5.   Notice how the mouse pointer has changed to a cassette tape, showing that the macro will now record all actions performed.

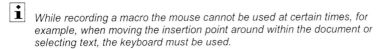 *While recording a macro the mouse cannot be used at certain times, for example, when moving the insertion point around within the document or selecting text, the keyboard must be used.*

6.   Carefully type the text: **Yours sincerely**, enter a few blank lines and your name.

7.   Select the **Stop Recording** button, , to end the recording.

*To record a macro quickly, double click **REC** on the **Status Bar** to display the **Record Macro** dialog box. Double click **REC** again to stop the macro recording.*

8.   Close the document <u>without</u> saving.

Driving Lesson 84 - Running a Macro

▣ Park and Read

Once a macro has been created and recorded, it can be run at any time.

☞ Manoeuvres

1. Open the document **Reservation**.

2. Move the insertion point to the place where the letter is to end.

3. Select **Tools | Macro | Macros**.

4. From **Macros in**, select All active templates and documents.

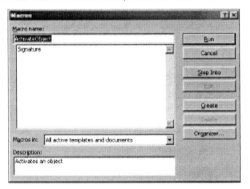

5. Click on **Signature**, then **Run** the macro.

6. Print the letter.

7. Close the document <u>without</u> saving.

Driving Lesson 85 - Copying a Macro

 Park and Read

It is possible to copy a macro so that it can be used in a different document.

Manoeuvres

1. Open the document **Bitesize**. This document contains a macro to print the page currently being viewed.

2. To copy the macro, select **Tools | Macro | Macros**. Click **Organizer**. The macro is to be copied to another document.

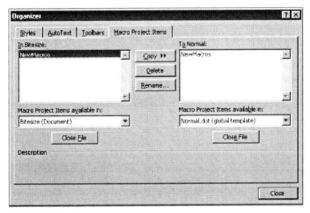

3. To copy the macro to the **PC** document, first click on **Close File** at the bottom right of the **Organizer**.

4. The button changes to **Open File**. Click on **Open File**.

5. From the **Open** dialog box, locate the data files, make sure **All Files** is selected from **Files of type** and select the **PC** document.

6. Click **Open**. In the **Organizer**, **NewMacros** should be highlighted in the **In Bitesize** area. Click the **Copy** button.

7. Click **Close**. When prompted, save the changes to **PC**.

8. Close **Bitesize** and open **PC**.

9. Move to page 3. Select **Tools | Macro | Macros** and select the **Printpage** macro, then click **Run**.

10. Close all documents without saving.

Driving Lesson 86 - Assigning a Macro to a Button

▣ Park and Read

The **Customize** dialog box can be used to assign a macro to a button on a toolbar. The button can then be added to any toolbar. The appearance of the button can also be changed. This can be done before or after the macro is recorded.

⌐ Manoeuvres

1. Start a new document and select **Tools | Customize**.

2. Click on the **Commands** tab and scroll down the list of **Categories** until **Macros** appears.

3. Click on **Macros** to view all the macros created.

4. Click and drag **Normal.NewMacros.Signature** up on to a toolbar. When the mouse is released a button appears.

5. Click on **Modify Selection** and in the **Name** box, enter **Signature**.

6. Click on **Change Button Image**.

Driving Lesson 86 - Continued

7.   Select the smiley face from the buttons.

8.   Close the dialog box and click the button to run the macro.

9.   Remove the button from the toolbar by holding **<Alt>** and dragging the button down off the toolbar.

10. To delete the macro, select **Tools | Macro | Macros**.

11. Select the **Signature** macro, then click **Delete**.

12. Select **Yes** at the prompt and click **Close**.

13. Close the document <u>without</u> saving.

Driving Lesson 87 - S.A.E.

This is a Self-Assessment Exercise, covering recording, running and copying macros and assigning a macro to a button. Try to complete it without any reference to the previous Driving Lessons in this section.

1. Open the document **E-commerce**.

2. Create a new macro to print the current page of a document, using menu selections.

3. Name the macro **Page**.

4. Run the **Page** macro.

5. Copy the macro to the **Shark** document.

6. Open the **Shark** document and move to page **3**.

7. Run the macro.

8. Close the document **Shark**.

9. On the **E-commerce** document assign the macro to a button. Select the eye button.

10. Run the macro using the new button.

11. Remove the button from the toolbar.

12. Delete the macro.

13. Close the document <u>without</u> saving.

If you experienced any difficulty completing this S.A.E. refer back to the Driving Lessons in this section. Then redo the S.A.E.

Once you are confident with the features, complete the Record of Achievement Matrix referring to the section at the end of the guide.

Index

Record of Achievement Matrix

This Matrix is to be used to measure your progress while working through the guide. This is a self assessment process, you judge when you are competent. Remember that afterwards there is an examination to test your competence.

Tick boxes are provided for each feature. 1 is for no knowledge, 2 some knowledge and 3 is for competent. A section is only complete when column 3 is completed for all parts of the section.

When all sections are completed in this way then you are ready for either a mock or the final examination.

	Date	Pass
Mock Examination		
Final Examination		

Tick the Relevant Boxes **1**: No Knowledge   **2**: Some Knowledge   **3**: Competent

Section	No.	Driving Lesson	1	2	3
1 Text Editing	1	Text Effects			
	2	Animated Text			
	3	AutoCorrect			
	4	AutoFormat			
	5	AutoText			
	6	Text Flow and Wrap			
	7	Text Orientation			
	8	Text Design: WordArt			
2 Paragraph Editing	10	Paragraph Shading and Highlighting			
	11	Paragraph Borders			
	12	Widows and Orphans			
	13	Creating Styles			
	14	Modifying Styles			
	15	Outline Level Styles			
3 Advanced Printing	17	Printing Odd or Even Pages			
	18	Printing Selected Text and Pages			
4 Document Layout	20	Adding/Deleting Section Breaks			
	21	Applying Section Shading			
	22	Multiple Column Layout			
	23	Modifying Column Layout			
	24	Modifying Column Width/Spacing			
5 Tables	26	Merging and Splitting Cells			
	27	Converting Text to Table			
	28	Sorting Table Data			
	29	Performing Calculations			
6 Text Boxes	31	Insert/Delete Text Boxes			
	32	Manipulating Text Boxes			
	33	Adding Borders and Shading			
	34	Linking Text Boxes			
7 Graphics and Drawing	36	Modifying Graphic Borders			
	37	Editing Graphics			
	38	Creating a Drawing			
	39	Aligning, Grouping and Layering Shapes			
	40	Creating a Watermark			
	41	Using a Drawing as a Watermark			

Tick the Relevant Boxes **1**: No Knowledge   **2**: Some Knowledge   **3**: Competent

Section	No.	Driving Lesson	1	2	3
8 Referencing	43	Creating Footnotes and Endnotes			
	44	Modifying/Deleting Footnotes/Endnotes			
	45	Note Options			
	46	Creating a Table of Contents			
	47	Updating a Table of Contents			
	48	Adding and Deleting Bookmarks			
	49	Cross-Referencing			
	50	Adding Numbered Captions			
	51	Automatic Caption Options			
	52	Creating an Index			
9 Templates	54	Creating a New Template			
	55	Modifying a Template			
10 Collaborative Editing	57	Adding/Editing Comments			
	58	Tracking Changes			
	59	Accept/Rejecting Changes			
11 Document Security	61	Password Protection			
	62	Removing/Changing Passwords			
12 Master Documents	64	Creating a Master Document			
	65	Creating a Sub-document			
	66	Adding/Removing a Sub-document			
13 Field Codes and Forms	68	Working with Field Codes			
	69	Editing and Updating Field Codes			
	70	Locking/Unlocking Fields			
	71	Creating and Editing Forms			
	72	Form Field Options			
	73	Protecting Form Fields			
14 Mail Merge	75	Editing a Data Source			
	76	Sorting a Data Source			
	77	Using Various Data Sources			
15 Working with Spreadsheets	79	Modifying a Worksheet			
	80	Creating and Positioning a Chart			
	81	Modifying a Chart			
16 Macros	83	Recording a Macro			
	84	Running a Macro			
	85	Copying a Macro			
	86	Assigning a Macro to a Button			

Other Products from CiA Training

If you have enjoyed using this guide you can obtain other products from our range of over 100 titles. CiA Training Ltd is a leader in developing self-teach and instructor led IT user-training materials.

Open Learning Guides

Teach yourself by working through them in your own time. Our range includes products for: Windows, Word, Excel, Access, Works, PowerPoint, Project, Lotus 123, Lotus Word Pro, Internet, FrontPage *and many more...*

We also have a large back catalogue of products, including PageMaker, Quattro Pro, Paradox, Ami Pro etc, please call for details.

Schools Editions

Specially written for older pupils, to be used by teachers, these guides integrate IT into the curriculum and take the pupil through the features of various software packages, with many revision exercises at the end of each section. Teacher's notes are included. Products include guides to Word, Excel, Access and Publisher.

Trainer's Packs

Specifically written for use with tutor led I.T. courses. The trainer is supplied with a trainer guide (step by step exercises), course notes (for delegates), consolidation exercises (for use as reinforcement) and course documents (course contents, pre-course questionnaires, evaluation forms, certificate template, etc). All supplied on CD with the rights to edit and copy the documents.

Purchasing Options

The above publications are available in a variety of purchasing options; as single copies, paper site licences or disk based site licences. However, Schools Editions are only available as paper site licences and Trainer's Packs are only available as disk based site licences.

Conventional Tutor Led Training

CiA have been successfully delivering classroom based I.T. training throughout the UK since 1985.

New products are constantly being developed, please call to be included on our mailing list.